Deliberative Policymaking

Deliberative Policymaking

Redesigning How We Make Education Policy

Elizabeth Grant

Harvard Education Press
Cambridge, Massachusetts

Paperback ISBN 9781682538838

Library of Congress Cataloging-in-Publication Data

Names: Grant, Elizabeth (School superintendent), author.
Title: Deliberative policymaking : redesigning how we make education policy / Elizabeth Grant.
Description: Cambridge, Massachusetts : Harvard Education Press, [2024] | Includes bibliographical references and index.
Identifiers: LCCN 2023053846 | ISBN 9781682538838 (paperback)
Subjects: LCSH: Education and state—United States. | Policy sciences—United States—Methodology.
Classification: LCC LC89 .G735 2024 | DDC 371.010973—dc23/eng/20240325
LC record available at https://lccn.loc.gov/2023053846

Published by Harvard Education Press,
an imprint of the Harvard Education Publishing Group

Harvard Education Press
8 Story Street
Cambridge, MA 02138

Cover Design: Wilcox Design
Cover Image: Sorbetto/via Getty Images
The typefaces in this book are Minion Pro and ITC Legacy Sans.

In honor of my mom, Sally,
who loved learning
and loved us

Contents

PART I

Redesigning Education Policymaking

CHAPTER ONE

Deliberative Policymaking

YEARS AGO WHEN IMAGINING education policymakers at work, I pictured a close-packed room of people sitting at a large conference table busy in deep and consequential discussions. I imagined it so clearly that when I applied for graduate work in education policy, I wrote on my application that I wanted to be at the table where policy decisions are made. At the time I was an elementary school principal. And the decisions that shaped the world in which our school operated—housing policy, resource allocation policy, and accountability policy, among others—were shaped by those at other tables. Many years after envisioning the circumstance, I had the opportunity to sit at the decision tables and hash out policy details with smart and passionate colleagues at the US Department of Education. It was a remarkable hands-on lesson in the complexities of making policy. Although as a team we were earnest and hardworking, we didn't always get the policy right. The puzzling question that got me started on this book is this: Why did we get it wrong when we had all the resources available to get it right? The process didn't need smarter and more experienced or thoughtful policy experts; they were available in abundance. Likewise, researchers and their contributions were accessible with a quick phone call. State and district educators similarly weighed in, sharing their local perspectives and real-world experiences. Still, and despite all of those resources, our team—and a plethora of policymakers before us—didn't get it right.

This is a book about education policy, yet it provides no easy remedy for teacher shortages, no quick fix for achievement gaps, and no lofty recommendations to advance equity. *Deliberative Policymaking* doesn't take on recent issues of pandemic-related learning loss, voucher programs, or safe and inclusive schools. The book does, however, speak to all of these issues by exploring questions essential to each: How might we create a fundamentally better way of making education policy decisions? My central argument is that we can improve education policy by improving our policymaking practices.

Through decades of attempts to reach educational excellence and equity across schools, we have put policies in place to improve outcomes, close achievement gaps, and increase access but have been frustratingly disappointed with how the achievements have not met our aspirations. In our quest for better policies, the style and quality of policymaking actions—the forward-moving processes we undertake to define public problems, determine a theory of change, create the conditions for implementation, and test policy approaches—have been neglected. Our search for answers relies on a style of policy analysis that identifies policy weaknesses, suggests options, and assesses an optimal choice. In the last couple of decades, evidence-based policymaking has elevated the importance of data and research and added a valuable tool to our policymaking toolbox. While these approaches are essential to improving education policies, they are insufficient.

One of the best business ideas I've heard lately is from a couple of friends who want to start a company called Hindsight Consulting; the tag line would be "Let Us Tell You What You Should Have Done." Though said tongue in cheek, the remark points out how often we have a wisdom when looking back that is not available when we look ahead. The natural problem-solving instinct is to critique what was done, why it was done that way, where it went wrong, and what ought to have happened. We have a lot of backward-looking analysis in education, yet few tools to move us from that point forward. In its current state, the policymaking process most leaders rely on is not fit to task. We may have the analytical skills to understand the problem and identify past mistakes, but we have few skills for working collectively to create better policies.

Take, for example, a promising policy that nevertheless overlooked implementation essentials. The Common Core State Standards initiative was meant to raise national learning expectations and ease cross-state comparisons. The standards were created through a well-considered process. Led by the National Governors Association and the Council of Chief State School Officers, the yearlong standards development work involved national organizations, content experts, K–12 teachers, and researchers and built from previous college- and career-ready standards efforts.[1] There were opportunities for public and expert feedback, and there was a validation committee to check the legitimacy of the standards.[2] Despite all that effort, Obama-era Race to the Top and No Child Left Behind waiver policies hastened implementation timelines and didn't account for the needs and opinions of some very important end users: classroom teachers and parents. States weren't given time to create the necessary infrastructure and materials to support teaching, build coalitions of supporters, and communicate objectives broadly. The whole Common Core implementation story is a complicated and largely political tale.[3] Still, policy decisions that missed users' needs and the challenges of implementation increased that political complexity and severely weakened national uptake of common learning standards. Common Core was rolled out in 2010, and by 2015 several states had reversed their adoption of the standards, and only a handful use the Common Core or related assessments today.[4]

In the chapters that follow, I argue that we can take purposeful action to rework policymaking activities so that they strengthen our collective capacity to arrive at and implement better policy. By its very nature, public policy, making rules for other people, is arrogant. My early vision of policymaking as a small group of people at a table was entirely accurate and, in hindsight, troubling. With few people involved, the process takes place amid a vast power differential between the governors and the governed. The response among those governing must be a humility regarding the wisdom of their ideas and also their positions of influence. A new approach to policymaking will not erase the power differential between decision-makers and citizens in terms of influencing policy, but it can reduce the gap and create a more even and accessible playing field. We can choose to engage in different policymaking practices.

The arguments here seek to rebalance how good education policymaking happens and calls for a far-reaching reconsideration of current federal and state education policymaking processes. The case is shaped by my experience working on federal policy issues and is illustrated with examples from federal and state policymaking. The focus is on changing policymaking practices at the federal and state levels. Yet, the lessons can shape policymaking generally. This book presses the reader to think differently about how we undertake policymaking by pushing past our current practice of getting a small group of smart people in a room with the hope that they come up with better ideas than those conceived by previous small groups of smart people. Yes, there must be good ideas, but the precursor to good ideas is good process.

EDUCATION POLICY CONTEXT

On a spring day in 1965, President Lyndon Johnson sat beside his elementary school teacher and signed the Elementary and Secondary Education Act (ESEA). Since that time the ESEA has shaped education-related federal policy and policymaking. The new federal leverage pushed states to provide greater education access and support to English learners, migrant children, and students with disabilities.[5] In partnership with the Civil Rights Act, the ESEA reshaped patterns of segregation and integration in public schools. Direct funding expanded state education agency capacity to oversee the federal dispersal of funds. The landmark legislation initiated powerful federal involvement in public elementary and secondary schools.

The ESEA also shaped education policymaking in multiple ways. First, like a magnet, the act drew policymaking energy and power to Washington, D.C. Conversations on education improvement and related policy are now largely driven from a national stage. Before the ESEA, local school boards were the primary point of policymaking, with their more incremental, conservative, and politically accountable decision-making.[6] Today, local school boards must contend with national conversations and federal policies. Second, the ESEA marks the rise of a professional class of education policymakers. The original law was influenced by a presidential task force of men drawn from universities, foundations, business, journalism, one state education agency, and one school district. The commissioner of education at the time, Francis Keppel, is said to have largely written the first draft of the law himself. The task force was a small elite group in 1965 whereas policy tables of today seat a large elite group more reflective of the size of federal policy influence. Third, the law highlighted the ever-present disconnect between policy and implementation. The chain of action from a federal agency to state agencies to local districts to schools and classrooms is long, and the links are weak. Early implementation studies noted how difficult it is to give directions from such a distance. These studies also highlighted the challenges of determining what behavior matters when there are vague or multiple policy goals, as in the ESEA.[7] In general, policymaking continues to neglect implementation considerations. Fourth, there is an underlying conflict between the timelines for reform held by politicians, policymakers, and practitioners. Measuring Title I impact was difficult because there were a number of ill-defined goals, as mentioned, and the timelines for expecting results were short. Politics demands quick feedback, while practitioners request time to implement new programs and change behaviors. Our timelines for measuring success are at odds with the reality of teaching and learning. Studies of early childhood education found that benefits accrued to program participants twenty years after participation in a high-quality intervention, and almost fifty years later researchers found benefits for the participants' children as well.[8] Our expectations, even today, don't allow a policy to take that long to make a difference.

The ESEA also highlighted tensions that are ongoing features of public education. The twin goals of educational excellence and equity split resources and attention when one becomes more important than another at any given time. Through its first decades the ESEA was focused on issues of equity as redress from socioeconomic disadvantage, discrimination, and language background, while in more recent decades the act emphasizes standards, assessments, and accountability in an effort to improve achievement.

Another tension exists between federal authority and state autonomy. The policy window for the ESEA was created by three developments of the time: a changing understanding of poverty, a new acceptance of federal support for schools, and the force of the civil rights movement.[9] Those political forces pulled power to the federal level. The policy window for the 2015 reauthorization of the ESEA returned some decision-making power to the states, but the original tension is ongoing. There also existed a tension between public education—publicly funded and publicly directed—and private education, represented by Catholic schools in large urban cities. In the ESEA this strain was relieved by deciding to use federal dollars to support children rather than institutions, thus avoiding direct public funding for private education though still sending money to private schools. Today that public-private tension is evident in privatization efforts such as vouchers and even in charter school conceptions.

In a similar vein, there has long been a tension in the purposes of education as a public good—serving the needs of community, civic responsibility, and citizenship—and a private good where the value of education accrues to the individual by increasing individual economic prospects. Today, the economic value of education also extends to issues of the nation's international competitiveness, as in the days of Sputnik. Multiple additional tensions play out in policymaking today: racial inequity, lack of minority representation, entrepreneurial agenda setting, nongovernmental actors, and extragovernmental funding, among others. They all create a "new policy equilibrium" even as the long-running tensions play on.[10] A new policymaking process would sit within this same context; it would not be exempt from these conditions. These features—the politics, the problems, the people, the policy cycle, and the tensions endemic in public education policymaking—shift with the times but endure.

The calls for better education policy endure as well. There are practical and political reasons for better policymaking, but the moral reasons for acting to change our practices should be upfront. The structures of education opportunity remain segregated, stratified, and unequal. School segregation has increased. Economic inequality has grown. Racial and socioeconomic achievement gaps remain. At the same time, education attainment is increasingly a marker of opportunity and success, a marker that is unevenly distributed. Opportunity for our children is structured by geography: where children live, the schools they attend, and the levels of poverty in their neighborhoods. We know that systemic factors such as these impact education outcomes differentially among children from rich and poor families. But new research approaches help us see that poor children who grow up in particular neighborhoods have sharply better odds of escaping poverty than similar poor children elsewhere.[11] Among the attributes of neighborhoods that increase social mobility are elementary schools with high test scores; this is another marker that is distributed unevenly.

A number of education trends were exacerbated by the COVID-19 pandemic. The disruption to schooling led to startling declines in learning.[12] As captured by the National Assessment of Educational Progress, referred to as the "nation's report card," there were sizable drops in the performance of nine-year-olds in math and reading, down to the levels from two decades ago.[13] Inequities grew too. The performance of low-achieving students, particularly low-income students and Black students, fell even more dramatically. The worrisome learning deficits are attributed to long-running school closures and the reliance on remote learning. Even before the pandemic, however, national tests in 2017 documented widening gaps, with scores for high-performing students increasing while those for low-performing students declined, possibly a consequence of the lingering effects of the Great Recession and uneven economic growth. The global pandemic has made even more stark the cascading effects of poverty and limited education opportunities, as its effects landed most heavily on particular groups.

Ironically, this complicated and uncertain moment may be the right time to reconsider and rethink how education policy is developed and evaluated. The pragmatic Deweyan ideas that emphasize democratic participation in education and a belief that "everyone is in the game" have never been more relevant.[14] Shifts in educational governance and a growing number of institutional players and influencers have dramatically changed the education landscape. The current Every Student Succeeds Act, the federal K–12 education law of the United States, is a good example. A foundational theme within the act is that education policy and practice will improve by decentralizing decision-making to the state level. By shifting the decision-making power away from the federal government and closer to the point of implementation, local policymakers can respond directly to the needs of their citizens. While the shift in geography may prove valuable, it does little to address the insufficiency of the policymaking process. Instead, the shift in power means that additional policymakers must know *how* to make good policy.

REDESIGNING EDUCATION POLICYMAKING

The ideas presented here are animated by my desire to design more effective education policies and improve education. I want to prompt better policymaking by turning attention to the way we choose to develop and design policies. Most problem solving relies on getting quickly to the right solutions and seemingly fails to consider the mechanisms of how we should be determining those solutions and developing related policies. Effective policy has been described in multiple ways: it solves the problem it aims to solve, it addresses a real need identified by educators, it is implementable because it has either the support or the infrastructure necessary, and the process is just and leads to a legitimate result.[15] All of these ideas are embedded in the aspiration of better policy, but at its most basic level effective policy is that which leads to better education outcomes for children. As policymakers, our primary aim will always be to make effective policy, and that in itself is a worthy accomplishment. Yet, we can expect more from education policymaking.

The manner in which we choose to make policy matters. The policymaking process can reflect the power and position of an elite set of actors and amplify only a small set of voices or can increase democratic participation, legitimize public decisions, and grow the civic capacity needed to take on and sustain education reforms that will better serve children. What we value in our policies is apparent as we variously reach for equity, excellence, or efficiency, for example. But in determining policymaking *practices*, we've not made those value choices as clear. We have neglected the role of values in education policymaking because we have assumed that our values are instantiated by the policies and the outcomes—the policies that work to open access, level the playing field, or equalize opportunity, for example—without consequent attention to how policymakers get to those hoped-for aims. Without an exploration of the values within our policymaking, we allow the effects of the process to be whatever they might be rather than recognizing that how we go about the work influences our choices and our outcomes while also shaping a broader system.

The spillover effects of policymaking are more consequential than we recognize, for good or for ill. For ill, policymaking can reinforce a reliance on centralized cadres of elite policymakers, sustain the gap between policy and implementation, and inhibit the restructuring of power and position frequently necessary for reform. For good, policymaking can be loaded with an expectation to serve democracy through deliberative processes that legitimize collective decisions and foster mutual respect and inclusivity. Policymaking can be expected to deepen social learning and cultivate conditions for successful implementation. Crucially, policymaking can generate "civic capacity," the community-wide understanding and mobilization that is necessary for education reform.[16] These aims require that we democratize policymaking activities. Two principles—civic capacity and deliberative democracy—must undergird policy activities to get more out of our policymaking.

Civic Capacity

Civic capacity is the ability of communities to collectively address public problems. The work of Clarence Stone, particularly his research with coauthors described in *Building Civic Capacity: The Politics of Reforming Urban Schools*, presents civic capacity as a foundation for education improvement.[17] Based on their research, Stone and his coauthors suggest that reform is built on communal and sustained civic effort that has the political wherewithal to upend traditional relationships and structures and to create new patterns and behaviors that will better serve schools. They assert that educational reform will not be successful without shared community knowledge that supports the collective action of multiple participants. Civic capacity represents the collective action requirements for successful education governance.

In a number of studies of urban education reform, the authors find that reform efforts are dependent on more than just a call to action; they also depend on a set of conditions that increase the likelihood of cooperation in a community problem-solving effort. For example, in the cities measured at the upper end of civic capacity—Pittsburgh, Boston, and Los Angeles—successful efforts weren't built on the charisma of a single person such as a superintendent, through the pressures of the business community, or on basic statements of community agreement. Rather, success was built on accumulating relationships, networks, resources, collaboration, knowledge, and active engagement over time. As Stone and his coauthors summarize, "The seeming lack of progress in reforming urban education is rooted neither in lack of motivation nor blanket resistance to new ideas, [and therefore] we are drawn to the conclusion that the key stumbling block is translating desire and ideas into cohesive, sustained, collective effort."[18]

More than just working together, the activities that create civic capacity rest on a foundation of shared understanding that is built together. Civic capacity is both civic mobilization and social learning. Stone argues that we must govern ourselves in the process of governing our efficient allocation of public goods to a diverse public. "If the public has a fragmented and superficial view of policymaking, then the democratic challenge is one of enabling the public to have a less fragmented and more sophisticated view of policymaking. It is for this reason that social learning, not efficiency, should be our central concern."[19] The creation of knowledge is a social phenomenon; it is "not just something *I* have; more fundamentally, it is something *we* have."[20] Civic capacity is the ability to continually generate that knowledge.

In looking again at the failings of Common Core implementation, it may be argued that shared learning ended when the process of standards development ended. The experts who were involved represented multiple constituencies but were relatively small in number, and though their learning was certain to have been great, it did not continue downstream to the end users at that deep level. Shared learning about why these standards were valuable, the reasons for emphasizing some standards over others, and the underlying agreements and compromises embedded within the choices were held by the few people involved at the front end. As the scholar Cynthia Coburn emphasizes in her look at consequential change, for an external reform to be implemented internally, there must be a shift in authority to those who are implementing the change and, importantly, a shift in knowledge.[21] Ownership of reform is contingent on the depth of knowledge held by those across the system; otherwise, the change isn't spread or sustained. The process of building civic capacity must be integrated into the process of policymaking.

Deliberative Democracy

The practices of civic capacity highlight the social requirements of democratic governance and are akin to John Dewey's ideas that our public processes must be democratic, deliberative, and educational.[22] Scholars Amy Gutmann and Dennis Thompson provide an overview of deliberative democracy theory and its practice in their book *Why Deliberative Democracy?*[23] In their explanation, deliberative democracy requires the justification of decisions through "reason-giving," an inclusive process in which we give one another mutually acceptable and generally accessible reasons in order to reach public decisions. What makes deliberative democracy deliberative is the discussion and justification through reasoning rather than through power. What makes it democratic is an expansive definition of who is included.[24] Democratic deliberation organizes political decision-making through persuasion, reason, argument, compromise, and, crucially, a shared public experience. In addition, deliberative democracy extends policy deliberation to people who normally are not part of the policymaking process.[25]

While Gutmann and Thompson's discussions represent the core arguments of deliberative democracy theory for the current volume, those arguments are pushed further by the work of "epistemic democrats" who move forward Dewey's ideas of social learning and democratic decision-making to emphasize that democracy is a learning process.[26] This tradition argues that in facing complex problems, a diverse collection of nonexperts does a better job than experts in solving the problems.[27] Essentially, collective decision-making is able to take advantage of what scholar Elizabeth Anderson describes as peoples' situated knowledge, tapping into the idea that citizens from different walks of life have different experiences of problems and policies, and because of that contribute important evidence to devising and evaluating solutions.[28]

Within this democratic tradition, the importance of deliberation and social learning is also presented in *The Power of Public Ideas*, a collection of essays edited by Robert Reich.[29] In Reich's volume the authors press policymakers to expand their responsibilities such that they engage the public in ongoing dialogue about problems, what's at stake, and our collective goals. A mistake with Common Core and many other efforts to improve public schooling was that policymakers did not recognize that democratic participation and public engagement—beyond simple policy communication—must begin early in the process and continue through implementation.

There is something fundamentally decent and good about respecting and including contributions from a broad spectrum of people's lived experience. And there are practical advantages to collectively identifying problems and collaborating in their resolution.[30] The arguments for that contribution to policy set up the direction of this book. Yet, this concept is more powerful and important than that of immediate practicality. Collaborative civic actions do not sit outside the hard truths of politics. I suggest that deliberative democracy offers an optimistic response to the contentious politics of our time. One way to address disagreement, discontent, falsehoods, and public distrust is to add more democracy, more civic engagement, more deliberation, and more social learning. Scholars of deliberative democracy argue that citizen deliberators can counteract elite manipulation of politics, overcome disadvantageous policy framing, avoid polarization, and make good decisions.[31] Deliberative policymaking in education is a fit for our time.

These theories and perspectives of civic capacity, social learning, and deliberative democracy are at the foundation of the approaches presented in the chapters ahead. The policymaking activities championed—using principles of human-centered design, harnessing the role of intermediaries, placing implementation at the forefront, and engaging in a new style of federal-state relations—push us to create the conditions for democratic participation and social learning in policymaking and to produce better policy decisions. My intention is not to provide a recipe for policy development but instead to present practical actions that are individually valuable in improving policy and that collectively address weaknesses in our current conceptions of policymaking. These four approaches hold the possibility of encouraging discussion, critique, improvement, and, importantly, new collective actions of policymaking.

CONCLUSION

The ideas I present in this book do not level the playing field upon which the governed and the governors enact policy, as there are multiple political and social interests that will continue to hold sway. Yet, the actions proposed can institutionalize democratic discourse and place the relational nature of education policymaking at the center. In altering our policymaking systems, we also alter the underlying conditions of the process. We affirm the virtues of a public education system in the manner in which we choose to improve that system.

It is important, however, to note some limitations to these arguments. First, these ideas evolved from experience with federal- and state-level policymaking and are focused on those activities. There are thousands of school districts across the country where policymaking occurs. While the ideas presented here may have value for considering education policymaking at a local level and may inform policymaking to address non–education-related public problems, I do not address those circumstances directly.

Second, the ideas for improved policymaking presented in the following chapters are grounded in these theories but do not extend them with new hypothesis and testing. I am making an analytical claim, not an empirical one. I do not present new evidence drawn from a research study of these concepts. Instead, I am positing a hypothesis that will require testing and refinement about what ought to be. While scholars suggest that careful institutional designs and multiple venues for deliberation, ones that are integrated with the political decision-making process, can secure positive effects, the full use of these ideas in education policymaking are new and untested. Therefore, they are open to contestation, deliberation, and further development.

The claims I make also acknowledge that democracy and civic capacity as well as the policymaking approaches presented ahead are not simple to achieve and consequently demand ongoing conscious effort. Without that effort they can become symbolic ideas rather than actions that improve education. Further, as scholars note, formalized actions of deliberative democracy such as forums, citizen surveys, and stakeholder meetings can be a technocratic response to weak governance rather than a radical people-led change; the formalized actions can be used to gain compliance with decisions rather than to drive different decision-making.[32] Processes themselves are not neutral; they embody particular values and biases and privilege some ideas over others. As such, they deserve as much critical attention as policies.

With all of this in mind, I encourage a reconsideration of education policy training. Policymakers are generally undertrained, and policy education is commonly underconceptualized. Policy programs typically educate students to analyze policy but not to craft policy. These programs rely on an economics-centered approach that doesn't attend sufficiently to deliberation and debate, local context and collaboration, the role of ideas, and implementation.[33] Programs that teach the forward-moving actions of making policy can focus on teaching how to move a policy to implementation, that is, to define the problem thoroughly and with local expertise, use evidence, engage in stakeholder partnerships, create coalitions, communicate strategically, and consider implementation ahead of policy development. Such programs can develop policymakers who will facilitate policy development instead of deciding among policy options themselves.

Political polarization, self-interest, hardened ideologies, time constraints, resource constraints, misinformation, and a host of other difficulties will continue to test the fortitude of policymakers. We are living in an age that will be noted for the rise of populism, the global pandemic, and a long-needed reckoning on race and racism. Public education has often been at the center of the maelstrom, dividing communities and testing the strength of both democracy and civic capacity. We've not yet tallied the impact of these events on how we manage our individual lives, let alone how we address public problems.

In the face of so much change and disruption, the ideas I lay out in this book are both serious and aspirational. The ideas are not a recipe for success as much as an invitation to think in different ways about how we conduct education policymaking and refine those practices. These ideas and propositions should be considered a work in progress.

Organization

The book is arranged in three sections. In the first section, this chapter and the next present the purposes of the book, the theories that guide my arguments, and the possibilities that are present in a redesigned policy process. Chapter 2 introduces the craft of policymaking and begins with an expansive understanding of who policymakers are and the opportunity at hand to cast familiar policy steps in a new light. The chapter sets up the central perspective on policy as our best guesses about improvement rather than as right solutions, a twist on our problem-solving approach that opens the process to social learning, civic capacity, and more deliberative approaches to the policymaking craft.

The four chapters in the second section are the heart of the book. Each chapter explores an alternative approach to better policymaking and ultimately to better education policy. These central chapters draw on policy theory, research findings, and recent education policy examples to illustrate how each approach can improve policymaking.

Chapter 3 frames policymaking within the principles of human-centered design. From empathy building to iterative prototype testing, the stages force policymakers' attention on people's needs, experiences, and preferences. The attitudes and practices of policy design thinking, along with its fundamental and generative emphasis on process, accompany us through the book.

Chapter 4 takes on the question of how to place implementation at the forefront of policymaking. I consider how we might move from the prevailing practice of implementation as faithfully executing policy to a revised view of implementation as social learning and continuous improvement.

Chapter 5 brings education intermediary organizations into a central policymaking role. The ask of policy intermediaries is that they take responsibility for not only supplying policy ideas but also creating and managing distinctive practices of public deliberation.

Chapter 6 presents a revised consideration of federal-state interactions that diminishes the hierarchical power struggle and emphasizes the reality and promise of shoulder-to-shoulder policymaking relationships.

The final section addresses implications of more deliberative policymaking. Chapter 7 links the arguments in this book to an expectation that future policymakers practice a new education statecraft and that policy training teaches those skills. Education policymakers need the expertise to facilitate deliberative policy development—in its most civic and democratic-minded iterations—and the skills to meet the moral, ethical, and democratic demands of public stewardship today.

Chapter 8 acknowledges the challenges in deliberative policymaking as it presses for engaging in new policymaking approaches. The manner in which we choose to make policy holds the possibility of increasing democratic participation, legitimizing public decisions, and growing the civic capacity necessary to take on and sustain education reforms that will better serve children. In summarizing the arguments made in the previous chapters, I press forward the importance of revitalizing and reshaping our policymaking processes.

CHAPTER TWO

The Art and Craft of Policymaking

IN THE SUMMER OF 1966, Senator Robert F. Kennedy traveled to South Africa at the invitation of a multiracial antiapartheid student association. He had been asked to speak at the annual Day of Reaffirmation of Academic and Human Freedom event. In an impassioned address, Senator Kennedy spoke of racial discrimination in South Africa and in the United States and of universal freedoms, human rights, possibilities for a more equitable future, and the necessity of protecting and preserving "the essential humanity of men."[1] Speaking specifically to a new younger generation of political and policy leaders, he warned against the dangers of futility, expediency, and timidity.

In perhaps the most memorable passage, Kennedy proclaimed, "Each time a man stands up for an ideal, or acts to improve the lot of others, or strikes out against injustice, he sends forth a tiny ripple of hope, and crossing each other from a million different centers of energy and daring, those ripples build a current which can sweep down the mightiest walls of oppression and resistance."[2] The speech was followed by a five-minute standing ovation. One of the student leaders later recalled that Kennedy granted nobility to their seemingly small and insignificant antiapartheid efforts and placed their work "back into the great sweep of history."[3] The passionate and challenging Day of Affirmation speech is considered his best.

The ability to strike a vision, draw people toward a cause, and harness ingenuity and hope in creating solutions to social problems is the art of policymaking. The artistic side of policy requires us to tap into our emotions and imagine a different and better world. On its own, however, the artistic side of policymaking falls short. Policymaking also requires craftsmanship.[4] Policymaking wants for skill and expertise gained through knowledge and practice, it demands hands-on political expertise, and it requires an understanding of education systems, political actors, and policy instruments.

In that memorable and soaring speech in South Africa, the ever-pragmatic Kennedy grounded his lofty ideas in the technical realities of policymaking, declaring that "idealism, high aspiration, and deep convictions are not incompatible with the most practical and efficient of programs."[5] In a remarkable era of hopes, dreams, and ambitious policymaking, Kennedy was a political realist and a policy craftsman. For years he had been deeply involved in the nitty-gritty of politics and policy. In the 1950s, he had served as a staff attorney on Senator Eugene McCarthy's anticommunist subcommittee, the campaign manager for John Kennedy's presidential bid, and then in the 1960s as the attorney general who federalized National Guard troops to integrate the University of Alabama. Joining the US Senate in January 1965, Robert Kennedy supported President Lyndon Johnson's Great Society programs and voted in favor of legislation on social security, voting rights, immigration, higher education, and housing and urban development. Yet, Kennedy was clear-eyed about the limits of policy. In a 1966 speech he raised the challenge of well-intentioned but ineffective government action. "There is not a problem for which there is not a program. There is not a problem for which money is not being spent. There is not a problem or program on which dozens or hundreds or thousands of bureaucrats are not earnestly at work. But does this represent a solution to our problems? Manifestly, it does not."[6] He brought that pragmatic approach to bear on education policy as well.

A year prior to the Day of Affirmation address, the Johnson administration's Elementary and Secondary Education Act (ESEA) was introduced in Congress. The bill was placed on a fast track and expected to move through Congress with few if any amendments. Yet, as the legislation moved toward a Senate vote, Kennedy saw a flaw and threatened to halt its quick progress. He was concerned that in spending Title I funds, school administrators would ignore the wishes and interests of poor families.[7] Kennedy is reported to have complained that "we really ought to have some evaluation in there, and some measurement as to whether any good is happening."[8] During a congressional hearing he remarked, "Obviously, I am in complete accord with the objectives of this bill. All I wonder is if we couldn't give further protection to the child by certain requirements?"[9] He wanted a measure of education progress. Kennedy saw evaluation as a tool of political accountability, a means to provide parents the information and thus the power they would need to ensure that Title I funds truly supported disadvantaged students.[10] In response to Kennedy's objections, an evaluation component was added to the bill, and the amended Elementary and Secondary Education Act became "the first major social legislation to mandate program reporting."[11] Kennedy's approach is instructive. Policymaking is about "tiny ripples of hope" as much as it is about politics, power, and technical requirements such as the evaluation of education program effectiveness. Kennedy was both a craftsman and an artist, and policymaking is a function of both.

This chapter is about the technical craft of making policy. I seek to ground abstract notions of policymaking in everyday language and explanations while also keeping some of their buoyancy. This chapter is not about how a bill becomes a law but rather how an idea comes to be an action, how it is developed, reshaped, codified, implemented, tested, and institutionalized.

Although I started the chapter with the compelling persona of Robert Kennedy, policymaking is not about a single great character; it is very much a collective action. To tell the story through individual decision-makers is incomplete and inaccurate. An emphasis on individual behaviors and actions puts policy in the realm of an elite few and out of reach for the rest of us. Yet, it is not out of reach; it is just unknown and unfamiliar. Policymaking does not reside in marble halls; it is at home everywhere.

A NEW DEFINITION OF POLICYMAKER

One way to move the focus from individual action to broader civic participation is to separate decision-making from policymaking. Though the two are often equated, policymaking is not a single choice but is instead the procedures and judgments that are part of a complicated and often very long process.[12] Our attention is drawn to the often-televised decision-making moment when a bill is voted into law, but that is a final step in the policymaking process. The earlier stages of defining the problem and crafting alternative options is the actual work of policymaking. Many more people are involved in the process of drafting policy alternatives than are involved in ultimate decision-making.

Who, then, are policymakers? Policymakers are a larger group than commonly recognized. The group includes many people who are in neither elected positions nor direct policy roles. To illustrate, I once worked for an advocacy organization known for its thoughtfulness and ingenuity in supporting community colleges. We were asked by US Senate staff to recommend legislative actions for President Barack Obama's $12 billion American Graduation Initiative. At the height of the Great Recession in 2009, the program was to be one of the president's signature initiatives intended to increase community college completion rates and, in the words of his announcement that summer, "offer training to millions of students who cannot afford four-year universities and opportunity to older workers who need new skills."[13] My colleague, a nationally respected advocate, and I wrote a memo hoping to shape the thinking of Senate staff and the direction of the legislation and spending. We were hopeful that we would have some influence but were surprised to see that the next version of the proposed bill included whole sections of our memo that had been copied directly into the legislative draft. It was remarkably satisfying to see our ideas get such attention yet startling to realize how detailed legislative language is often written. The Senate staff weren't experts on community college issues and needed to look elsewhere. My colleague had that expertise, and it was smart to solicit his input. Still, it was unexpected that they would use our language directly. In that experience, I recognized the extent that policy ideas and even legislative language are developed outside the government policy apparatus. For that moment, my colleague and I were policymakers.

A revised view of policymaking starts with a revised perspective on who policymakers are. Across the stages of policymaking as we move from idea to implementation, a seemingly small group of policy actors in capital cities hold sway from top positions in government. It is important, however, to separate the roles of policy deciders and policy contributors. Often, those who decide on the legislated version of policy have done little to actually shape that policy. In this book I define policymakers as those who supply policy ideas, language, or reasoning to decision-makers. Those who supply policy ideas include a much broader pool of people including those in advocacy groups and think tanks, philanthropy, government agencies, nonprofit organizations, and research firms as well as school board members and educators who are teaching and leading in schools. There is no limit to the size or positions of those who, under the right circumstances, can supply policy ideas. They may not have decision-making power, but they shape policy all the same.

On the other side of the equation from those who supply policy ideas are those who can demand better policy. This group primarily includes those in legislative and executive decision-making positions. Both groups can act to improve policymaking. By insisting on better policy development processes, those on the demand side can use their positions to question how policies are developed and raise expectations that policy options are more thorough, user-centered, ground-up, implementation-ready, and directed at well-defined needs.

In this book, policymakers are conceived as those who supply policy ideas, language, or reasoning to decision-makers. Their input and expertise inform and influence the policymaking process and undergird the actions of legislators and executive-level leaders. I focus on the actions and beliefs of this broader group of policy actors because they supply policy ideas and a broad range of perspectives. It is this larger collection of policymakers who will create better policy development practices.

In the sections below I introduce basic policy definitions and tools as a foundation for later discussions about improving the process. I start with a discussion of public policymaking and the commonly recognized policy cycle. Though the policy terms and ideas are fundamental and familiar, I aim to tell a slightly different story about the policy process as a whole and the particular steps of problem definition and implementation within that larger policymaking process. This chapter introduces the notion that policy is better seen as our best guess for how to solve a problem rather than as the solution itself. The section then speaks to politics and works to tease apart policy from politics even as they are, in truth, well entwined. The chapter concludes with an overview of education policymaking themes that have been part of the policy conversation across decades.

PUBLIC POLICYMAKING

Policy is a set of rules or guidelines that determine a course of action. Policy is as official as regulations, laws, ordinances, and court decisions and as informal as common practices. Policy can take the form of implemented programs or procedures as well. And, importantly, policy can also be inaction, or the decision not to address an issue or problem.[14] The choice not to formally address a problem is a de facto policy decision as well.

To capture the abstract concept of policy, it is useful to see policy in everyday life. Policies show up as rules in everything from speed limits to condo association bylaws to municipal recycling ordinances to the human resource policies within businesses. Policies are apparent in programs that provide breakfast at schools and new reading curricula. Policies can drive grand changes but are also present in small education procedures we adopt such as the start and end times of a school day and the requirements for registering students within particular districts or school boundaries.

Policymaking happens too in the private sphere of family life. In fact, it can be helpful to picture the cycle of policy activities in the familiar setting of the family. Parents commonly struggle to create and implement effective policies around children's bedtime or the use of electronic devices at the dinner table. Whether within a family, a private business, or in public, the first step in the process is to recognize and describe a problem, then put it on an agenda to deal with. The policy is then drafted, adopted, and implemented. If the policy process continues, we evaluate the policy and, based on an assessment of effectiveness, possibly start the cycle again by reconsidering the problem in order to improve the policy. In the family context, parents revisit and refine bedtime policies over and over in the search to find something that works. These same actions that happen in the family are carried out in developing any new policy, whatever the context. Although the process doesn't travel a straight line and rarely progresses from one step to the next as pictured in the well-known policy cycle, the journey of an idea from early development to implementation includes each activity represented in that cycle: problem identification and definition, agenda setting, policy formulation, adoption, implementation, and evaluation.

The simplicity and ubiquity of the policy cycle steps, present in one form or another in much of our everyday decision-making, provides an easy touchstone for considering the more complex and politically laden process of public policymaking. Public policymaking is unique from other forms of policymaking. Public policies are decisions made by those who have governance responsibilities. This is key. Public policymaking is the action of making rules for others. This wide reach gives public policymaking a unique power and, consequently, must elicit among policymakers a self-conscious humility. Public policies create burdens along with benefits and therefore have moral and ethical repercussions. In truth, policymaking is an attempt to change peoples' behaviors, beliefs, and actions. Further, the rules devised through public policymaking—at a federal, state, or district level, for example—typically impose a cost on others rather than on ourselves. Few people in governing positions will live under the welfare rules they create or the testing conditions they impose on schools. State and district education leaders may not have children in the schools that are subject to their accountability policies. Governing policymakers rarely are involved in policy implementation where policy is edited and molded as it plays out in unique contexts.

Public policies are moral actions in another sense as well: they are a course of action that we choose when we might have chosen differently.[15] Public policymaking is the determination of one action over another, the assertion of one set of values or beliefs over another, the victory of one idea over another that might have equal claim to furthering progress and improvement.

Those familiar with the policy cycle will not see new steps in the chapters that follow but will see a shift in view that argues for greater emphasis on problems and implementation as well as more attention to seeing and refining the process as a whole. Policymaking must be participatory, and it is in the early problem-definition stage that there is room for participation and in the later implementation stage that there is an expectation of participation. The sections below describe these steps and highlight their importance to deliberatively democratic practices and the social learning requisite for civic capacity. It is at these two points in the policymaking process where the community can most readily participate. Legal expertise may be required to write policy language, political position is required to enact it, and research skill is required to evaluate it, but determining the problems and implementing solutions are not limited to a small elite. An argument can be made that public participants are able to frame problems in ways that break from professional conceptions and attend to their values and needs while bringing the ingenuity, know-how, and resources to implementation that may improve public actions.[16]

Better policymaking requires organizational arrangements and mechanisms that increase participation—design thinking practices and a learning infrastructure, for example—and that increase the knowledge and skills of nonelite policymakers and hence their power within the process. In a famous discussion of social movements, scholars Frances Piven and Richard Cloward note that people cannot alter the institutions "to which they have no access, and to which they make no contribution."[17] Placing greater attention on problem definition and implementation not only improves policy actions but also rearranges access to the systems of policymaking.

Problem Definition

The power of problem definition is too often overlooked. Problem definition is the act of discovering a problem, assigning causation or failure, and identifying a target population that is the focus for improvement efforts or behavior change. Problem definition holds within it the assumptions, value judgments, and causality that frame ensuing debate.

How we define a problem determines how we think about it. Problem definition labels a condition, such as climate change, as a problem.[18] The way we define that problem puts us on a path toward a set of solutions. By defining the problem as A, we have A-related solutions to choose from; if we define the problem as B, we look to B-related solutions. Climate change provides an example. If we define the problem as that of individual choices, our solutions will seek to shape individual choices around recycling or biking to work, for example. However, if we define the problem as one of systemic effects, the solutions will revolve around regulating the emission of greenhouse gases or incentivizing electric car production. The definition, then, determines the subsequent policy options that are available to solve the defined problem. Problem definition opens some policy pathways while closing others.

Like a window frame that determines the boundaries of what we see, a particular problem frame sets the parameters within which the policy is decided. That initial step in the policy process anchors the problem within a set of assumptions and beliefs that shape future actions and reshape the landscape for later policy. Within the definition is the cause of the problem. For example, education underperformance can be attributed to any of a number of challenges: insufficient resources, limited preschool preparation, poverty, racial inequity, poor leadership, and so on. Under Secretary Arne Duncan, the US Department of Education defined low-school performance as a school-based problem that required comprehensive school turnaround effort. The problems that needed to be addressed within turnaround schools included poor school leadership, ineffective teaching, and insufficient rewards or professional development for staff, among other challenges. Based on this diagnosis, the School Improvement Grant program then offered up to $2 million per school to implement specific actions such as replacing teachers and leaders, restarting schools in a new form, or closing them all together. Across the country, the solutions that followed from that problem definition affected cities, neighborhoods, teachers, and leaders. As the political scientist John Kingdon explains, "There are great political stakes in problem definition. Some are helped and others are hurt, depending on how problems get defined."[19] The act of defining a problem is political and consequential.

One reason for this is that how the problem is defined determines how the story is told, and once that storyline is codified in policy it becomes the paradigm through which we see the world and conduct business. It is particularly important to attend to the problem definition step as we look at improving the full policymaking process. The fundamental challenge of policymaking—and perhaps the most politically consequential action—is defining the problem. And for each problem there is no objectively correct definition. Problems are defined by how we see the world and where we sit within systems. They are neither right nor wrong. Community agreement on the problem and its definition establishes the foundation for sustained improvement and institutionalizing lasting practices. Consequently, the definition must be negotiated. As urban scholar Clarence Stone and his colleagues contend in their work on civic capacity, "Only where communities share a common perspective on the problem facing them is major reform likely to be put into place and kept in place."[20] Agreement on the problems allows multiple parts of the education and civic communities to pull in the same direction toward solutions.

The policy improvement actions I am proposing are grounded, in one way or another on problem definition. Design thinking is fundamentally about designing a problem so well that the solution works. Implementation is about understanding the context of the problem so well that there is relevant room in the policy for street-level adaptation. The proposed role of intermediary organizations is largely that of working collectively with communities to define problems. Reimagining federal-state relations is meant to facilitate a shared understanding of problems across levels of government and a collaborative responsibility for solving them.

It takes time and attention to define a problem well. Albert Einstein is credited with saying "If I were given one hour to save the planet, I would spend 55 minutes defining the problem and five minutes resolving it." This wonderful reframing turns on its head our regular practice of jumping quickly to solutions. As policymakers, this is the point in the process where we should want to spend the most time.

Implementation

When ideas and events come together, through either the outside force of a focusing event or the internal efforts of leaders and advocates, a window of opportunity is opened for policy to move forward. A change in administration, a crisis, sustained media attention, and even the ascendance of a powerful idea over time can focus decision-makers' attention and create opportunities for policy change. John Kingdon suggests that a policy window is created when three "streams"—problems, politics, and a policy response—flow together.[21] Often, unusual events focus attention on particular problems and create the political conditions necessary to move forward.

Implementation is often regarded as everything that happens after a policy is adopted, but that mindset has limited the impact of many well-intentioned policy decisions. Policy design and policy implementation are considered discrete and distinct stages rather than an integrated process.[22] Because implementation is seen separately from policymaking, it is rarely considered at the front end of the process. In the policymaking process we spend too little time and effort looking forward to implementation.

Since the large-scale implementation of education policies in the 1960s, researchers have studied implementation barriers and struggles and have produced a rich and coherent body of literature. Implementation includes communication processes that explain policy to those who are involved in its implementation, technical assistance, and capacity-building activities necessary to begin something new as well as the actual work of changing actions and behavior at the grass roots, or street level. To implement policy is to put a decision into effect and attend to it over the course of time. There are a number of lessons to draw from implementation research—policymakers can't mandate what matters, successful implementation is contingent on capacity and will, support combined with pressure is essential, and systemic improvement requires both bottom-up and top-down change—yet these lessons are rarely considered by those who design and draft policy.[23]

In an early analysis of the distance between policy and practice, David Cohen and James Spillane argue that the efforts of instructional reform "might have more chances of success if the entire venture were conceived and executed as a great educational enterprise, one in which state and national leaders had as much to learn as teachers and students."[24] Policymaking is a learning process. Later work by Spillane and colleagues suggests that implementation hinges on social understanding and the process of making sense of policy in order to change practice.[25] Sense making is a communal rather than individual activity and requires levels of public engagement and communication that are unusual in policymaking. If implementation is dependent on shared understanding, then implementation is not just service delivery; it is coconstruction.[26] Thus, sense making requires continued learning among policymakers and implementers. Policy might then include within itself a way of learning to improve and an infrastructure—feedback loops, deliberative forums to build knowledge, and extended time frames to study results—to facilitate that improvement.

Raj Chetty, an economist and the director of Opportunity Insights at Harvard University, argues that successful implementation requires learning over time by paying attention to the details of end-line service delivery.[27] In examining federal housing data, he and his colleagues noted that most low-income families who received housing vouchers facilitating the move to higher-opportunity neighborhoods chose not to move. Uncertain about the reasons, they experimented with providing different supports and information and found that if they designed the program just a little differently, if they provided assistance in finding housing in the higher-opportunity neighborhoods and help in navigating the rental process, the number of families making the move increased from 15 percent to 60 percent. As Chetty says, programs have a fundamentally different effectiveness if policymakers learn and design programs in a little better way.

Policymakers typically leave the difficulties of implementation to the implementers to sort out at the tail end of the process. Instead, they must recognize that democratic participation and public engagement—beyond simple policy communication—must continue through implementation.

Chapter 5 explores how we might consider implementation during the early stages of policymaking as well as the later stages. What would it mean to build social learning into the policy process? How might policy rules and regulations provide implementation support while also pressing for change? How might policies build implementation capacity and civic capacity as they create new practices?

Policy Cycle

Though depicted as a simple cycle, the path to policy is rarely sequential. Rather than moving step by step, policy development often follows a pattern of two steps forward and one step back. For example, after defining the problem and placing it on the decision agenda, the struggle to write an effective policy theory of action might require going back to reconsider or reframe the problem definition. At the implementation step, real-world challenges may require returning to and reinterpreting the written policy. Properly evaluating a policy requires understanding the original problem as it was defined and the policy intent as it was captured in the policy formulation. In addition, the cycle as portrayed gives each of the six steps equal billing, although in reality some are given more attention than others.

Though the policy cycle doesn't capture important nuance or complexity, the metaphor provides a framework for seeing each individual step and at the same time seeing the process as a whole. What matters is understanding the complexity within each step and therefore the possibility for improvement within each action. Through decades of research on policy and politics, there is a rich literature that details the activities in the policy cycle and explains how they unfold under different conditions. Our task now is to consider these steps within the framework of building civic capacity and anchoring actions in deliberative democracy. Each step provides an opportunity to undertake more inclusive, democratic actions or add greater public engagement or deliberation. The picture of the cycle also helps in seeing opportunity across the whole process. The cycle as a whole should be seen as carrying within it a grander opportunity than just reaching a good policy at the end but also the larger responsibility of building capacity for education reform.

POLICY AS HYPOTHESIS

Policy takes on the formality of a conclusion when enacted as law and thus feels solid and immovable. We know from our understanding of implementation that this is far from true, and yet we commonly approach policymaking as if in search of solutions, elusive silver bullets that will cut through complexity and solve problems. Title I of the ESEA was established as compensatory funding for disadvantaged students in a fight against poverty. Policymakers at the time did not fully consider the distance between the causes of poverty and the power of schools to create social change. As one congressional staff member remarked, the assumption was that "all you needed to do was give [educators] some tools and some dollars and good things would happen."[28] Early evaluations of ESEA implementation documented the slippage between policy intent and local practice and served to diminish 1960s-era optimism about the role of education and schools in reducing poverty.[29]

A contrary way to approach the process is to explicitly consider policy as hypothesis. A hypothesis is tentative, an educated guess with a number of assumptions, suppositions, and arguments based on data, intuition, or experience. To describe policy as hypothesis takes it out of the realm of certainty and gives it a more experimental nature that can be tested and improved rather than set in stone. John Dewey emphasized this approach almost a century ago, arguing that our ideas and views on policies and programs ought not be frozen in place but instead constantly shaped and tested. He proposed that "policies and proposals for social action be treated as working hypotheses, not as programs to be rigidly adhered to and executed."[30] Dewey's idea was that policies be entertained to the extent that they are subject to both constant evaluation and revision.

Despite efforts to use research to increase our certainty about policy solutions, policy will never be fully evidence-based. The foundation of the policy may rest on a well-substantiated theory, but the policy itself is a hypothesis of how to put that theory into practice. Take early childhood education as an example. Educators today work off the well-established theory that high-quality early childhood education pays off over the course of a lifetime.[31] Nevertheless, any single early childhood policy is a hypothesis of how to support such programs, scale them up, or make them universally accessible. As one summary report on the evidence suggests, "Policymakers can be highly confident that well-designed and well-implemented early childhood programs can improve the lives of children and their families."[32] The trick in policymaking, then, is to make sure that the programs are well designed and well implemented. The theory of early childhood education's importance has been tested, and there is verifiable data backing up the conclusions, but the policy implemented through government and agencies and educators take us back to a starting point: it is a hypothesis about how to run a program based on a theory. Construing policy as hypothesis rather than solution opens up new ways of designing policy and measuring success.

The subtle shift in thinking may make a big difference in our policy decisions. What might it mean for how we design the process? Perhaps it would mean that we put forward the best, most thoughtful evidence-informed policies knowing that they will require improvement over time and build that process in from the beginning. It might mean that policy would be done side by side with research, that we would test our hypotheses deliberately rather than doing them one at a time: research, then policy, then more research, and more policy. It might mean that we double down on evaluation and spell out within the policy an approach to gathering feedback and making improvements. It might even mean that implementation would be supported as part of the hypothesis test—it would be built into the testing conditions—rather than seen as a separate process.

In his book on describing a physician's work, the doctor and writer Atule Gawande comes surprisingly close to describing the task of policymaking, albeit in the language of medicine. "As a doctor, you go into this work thinking it is all a matter of canny diagnosis, technical prowess, and some ability to empathize with people. But it is not, you soon find out. In medicine, as in any profession, we must grapple with systems, resources, circumstances, people—and our own shortcomings, as well. We face obstacles of seemingly unending variety. Yet somehow, we must advance, we must refine, we must improve."[33] Policy too can be seen as in need of improvement from the start. As Gawande argues, it is the process of getting better that matters. An effective policy, then, is one that shifts or ameliorates the problem rather than being held against the measuring stick of solving the problem. We are not aiming for perfection; we are aiming for something better. The approaches in the chapters that follow suggest how we might get better at making and implementing effective education policies.

POLITICS AND POLICYMAKING

Policymaking is threaded through with politics. It is not possible to separate these threads, but it is useful to distinguish between the two. In basic terms, politics is the practice of governance and the exercise of power, status, or authority; policy is the rules we create through politics. Politics is commonly presented and often seen as the pushing and shoving between political parties or as the action that mangles good policy ideas in an ugly sausage-making process. But there is a positive view of politics as an "activity *out of the ordinary*" when we come together for the common welfare and act on it.[34] Politics is how we sort out community interests and values, the opinions of our present and the visions of our future. The word "politics" derives from the ancient Greek word *pōlis*, meaning "city-state" or "body politic." The *pōlis* is both the community of individual citizens and their collective purpose. Likewise, politics is about the pursuit of both individual and collective goods. Politics is concerned with the shape of any human community and is about shaping that community; thus, politics matters in shaping our education policy processes as well as the ultimate forms of our education systems.

Politics shapes public institutions and public ideas, yet there have long been calls to remove politics from education policy.[35] Based on their civic capacity research, Stone and colleagues observed that "America spent most of the twentieth century trying to take politics out of education. That was a mistake."[36] Their argument for going through rather than around politics is that education reform doesn't happen without the energy of politics. Reform doesn't stick without the political forces that create lasting "institutional legacies" in both relationships and organizations.[37] Political action creates public understanding of the many possible visions for policy and broadens the range of our responses.[38] Even in highly partisan times, where the political world appears dysfunctional and political interactions are charged to the point of violence, to remove politics would remove the deliberation, negotiation, and legitimacy from policy decision-making. These scholars don't minimize political challenges; instead, they contend that education reform is so deeply political that it takes masterful command of community relationships, coalition building, and bridge building to mobilize collective action. The education successes in the Chicago Public Schools are attributed in large part to the political alliances and partnerships that formed across businesses, philanthropy, reform organizations, colleges of education, and nonprofit organizations, creating a "civic architecture" that supported years-long improvement efforts.[39] El Paso's educational improvements too relied on political partnerships to create the formally organized and staffed Collaborative for Academic Excellence initiative that combines institutional bases of power and resources—school districts, the university, the community colleges, the state, the county, the city, and the chamber of commerce—along with parent and community leadership and grassroots engagement.[40] Both the problems and the solutions to educational improvement lie within the political realm.[41]

In addition, removing politics cedes the policymaking space to those currently in positions of power. For decades, communities of color and of lower socioeconomic status have seen the minimization of politics in education as a "smokescreen for elite, white rule."[42] Removing politics from education reduces minority power to affect change. Elite power is about maintaining position and convincing citizens that this is the way "normal" democratic politics work as much as it is about particular policies.[43] Elite policymaking power relies on the advantages of knowledge, institutions, expertise, and entrenched positions.[44] John Dewey wisely notes that these positions separate experts from a democratic public, and as experts become a specialized class "they are shut off from knowledge of the needs which they are supposed to serve."[45] It becomes impossible for those in elite positions to secure the knowledge needed to frame policies properly and to meet the genuine interests of society. Consequently, elite policymaking reduces the educative features of democratic government, the clarification of common interests through public discussion. As Dewey explains, "a class of experts is inevitably so removed from common interests as to become a class with private interests and private knowledge, which in social matters is not knowledge at all." The essential need, Dewey explains, is to improve our processes of inquiry, debate, discussion, and persuasion.

In a few short years, however, we have entered a new policy landscape in which the spread of technology and networking and a new generation discontented with limits on their participation are changing the structure of power.[46] Massive social movements such as Black Lives Matter and Me Too, the rise of populist politics, and the global COVID-19 pandemic mark a transition point. Power has been traditionally held among few people or institutions by virtue of what they know or own or control.[47] Politics is about the distribution of power, and we are living through shifting political times. There is a new contestation of power among individuals and groups that will affect policymaking going forward. Some observers describe this as the rise of new power, the power of broad participation and collective action.[48] As the feminist writer Carolyn Heilbrun wrote, power is the ability to take one's place in the discourse that is essential to action and the right to have one's part matter.[49]

There are multiple ways to understand power and its use. Attention to power, as presented in the pages that follow, is not the power of the classic definition of power over others—that A has power to make B do something that B wouldn't do—but instead is the definition of power that asserts that A has the power to advance A's interests. This alternate form of power, as described by the government and democracy scholar Archon Fung, is about protecting interests—by organizing, collecting allies, and raising issues to public view—rather than bending the will of others.[50] When we consider options for education change, it is important to look beyond more apparent forms of power and toward other forms of power that set the conditions for social change. This understanding of power draws from age-old power dynamics regarding the provision of benefits and the imposition of burdens, but it allows for multiple ways to meet A's interests. This version of power derives from the importance of ideas and values, of relationships and organizing, of negotiating ways to meet interests without the win-lose contest of ceding or winning power. For example, an emphasis on the power to shape policy allows for a new look at federal-state relations that doesn't set the contestation on the playing field of domination but instead looks to how power can be used and shared to encourage that both federal and state interests are met rather than that one dominates the other.

New power dynamics will require that the governing elite genuinely share power.[51] This idea implies that federal agencies share policy decision-making power with state and district agencies, that states share with districts, and that all share with community members. This is not a smooth process. As Frederick Douglass clearly explained, power concedes nothing without a demand. Yet, new power expectations that value direct participation, transparency, and collaboration are forcing change in the business world and may yet do the same in the realm of governance. This book sits in the new power camp. The ideas presented push forward with approaches that further new power structures and encourage change in the underlying structures of power in education policymaking.

CONCLUSION

Politics and the analysis of power is not the focus of this book; instead, they are underlying conditions that animate the concerns and recommendations presented. Policy books commonly give attention to the political interactions among policy players, the distribution of power and interests among constituencies, and how politics shapes policy. This book acknowledges these forces yet attends to policy approaches that even in today's partisan context can mitigate some of the power that politics has over good policy ideas. By this, I mean that the actions embedded in the four approaches—human-centered design, the role of intermediaries, an implementation focus, and the dynamic interconnections in federal-state relations—are each at some level about power distribution. And each seeks to find new arrangements that increase democratic participation and civic capacity.

Given these conditions, the question ahead is how we can be more successful in designing effective policy and in the similarly monumental task of creating a new shape for our community built on civic capacity and deliberative democracy. There are multiple reasons, most of them rational, that explain policy challenges. Our political organization rewards passing legislation over the work of implementing that legislation. Democracy demands compromise. The education system is fragmented across layered levels of government that complicate coordination and disperse both authority and responsibility. Policymaking is fraught with constraints and failures. It is understandable that Robert Kennedy warned against the dangers of futility and expediency, the concern that we will toss our hands in the air or take the convenient path when other paths hold greater promise along with greater risk. Yet, he also warned of the danger of timidity and argued for courage to change the world. Kennedy grounded this idealistic aim with the pragmatic crafts of governance and policymaking. With those aims in mind, the next chapters focus on how we might hone the policymaking craft in order to reach these goals.

PART II

New Policymaking Practices

CHAPTER THREE

Policy Design Thinking

THE AERON OFFICE CHAIR has been called the best-selling office chair on the planet.[1] It is sleek, modern, and curvy. The Aeron is such a groundbreaking and aesthetically beautiful design that it was added to the permanent collection of the Museum of Modern Art in New York City. Yet, development of the Aeron did not begin as an art project or an office chair project. Surprisingly, the groundbreaking chair grew out of a ten-year effort to design functional furniture for the elderly.[2]

In the 1970s two designers, Bill Stumpf and Don Chadwick, were hired by the Herman Miller company to create a new line of furniture for older adults. The lounge chair had become the center of elderly people's universe, as they sat in hospital recliners for dialysis or spent hours in them watching TV.[3] The designers set out to create a better chair to serve those needs. Rather than starting with a redesign of current chairs, the designers took the unusual steps of first discovering what people wanted and needed. To do this they listened to those who were going to use the chair. They visited residential facilities and retirement homes and watched people get in and out of chairs. They spoke to physical therapists, ergonomic specialists, and geriatric specialists. They heard users explain that the reclining lever was difficult to use, the thick foam cushions became uncomfortable over time, and the leather and vinyl coverings trapped body heat. Capturing this type of information was unusual. As one of the project leads said, "These sorts of realizations at the time weren't just overlooked, they weren't [deemed] important."[4]

Deeming the user experience important sets human-centered design apart from typical development and decision processes. As designer Bill Stumpf later said, "Truly great design has never existed apart from the human condition."[5] In direct response to the very human conditions of the elderly and the sick, his design team experimented with an easy-recline mechanism and invented a breathable fabric framework that would prevent heat buildup and pressure points. Though the new chair was never sold to customers, its features were the starting point for the innovative Aeron launched in 1994. In addition to being artistically interesting, the Aeron broke from more traditional practices of using wood frames, foam cushions, and upholstery, instead using a breathable mesh fabric, molded plastic, and ergonomic shapes.[6] Today, the chair is an often-copied icon of design and usability.

Human-centered design, or design thinking, is a creative problem-solving method that emphasizes innovation, iteration, and the needs of the end user. As one veteran designer explained, human-centered design is "an approach that puts human needs, capabilities, and behavior first, then designs to accommodate those needs, capabilities and ways of behaving."[7] There are multiple versions of the design process, but each typically includes the four steps of discovery, idea generation (ideation), prototyping, and testing. The simplicity and adaptability of this solving-problems approach encourages its use beyond the physical design of products to the design of procedures, rules, structures, and services.

One way to view design thinking is as a tool of innovation. Through the design process we can brainstorm our way to radically new ideas and undiscovered solutions. It is this characteristic that has placed the design process so centrally to the industrial arts. Yet another way to characterize design thinking is as a decision-making process. This version of the tool emphasizes the front-end work of empathy building and the back-end work of iteration and testing. Design thinking in the early stages of a project can directly respond to the complexity of the problems addressed, along with their interconnected variables and dependencies, and provides continual allowance for refining decisions over time and with new input from formal and informal feedback loops.

Human-centered design is used to create technology that is more user-friendly, deliver services more attuned to user needs, and build products with greater consumer appeal. Increasingly design is being used to refine implementation of government programs and to collaboratively improve classroom instruction. However, human-centered design is not commonly used to develop policy.

As a frame for education policymaking, the design process helps policy actors recognize the complicated realities intrinsic to educational settings and place human needs and capabilities first. This chapter introduces the ideas of design theory and how they can be applied to the policy process. Design thinking is not the single answer to multiple policymaking challenges, but it does provide a formal human-centered problem-solving process that can bolster civic approaches to policymaking, as it attends to the context and conditions of education challenges and builds feedback into the process. And though design thinking can lead to Silicon Valley–style innovation, its value goes further as a tool with the possibility to deepen social learning, legitimize collective decisions, foster mutual respect and inclusivity, build civic capacity, and cultivate conditions for successful implementation.

The underlying logic of design thinking as decision-making is in many ways fundamentally different from that of the rational model of decision-making. Design thinking is a process of exploration embedded within a decision structure.[8] Contemporary policymaking follows a rational approach: define the problem, identify alternative solutions, establish evaluative criteria, analyze the alternatives, and make a decision. The process stops at the decision point and does not include implementation. It is a commonsense model that we consciously or unconsciously follow in most education policymaking today. As with any model, rational decision-making requires that certain assumptions hold in order to make it work. The rational model assumes high-quality or "perfect" information for making a decision, measurable criteria by which to judge among alternatives, and the time and resources to evaluate the alternatives properly. All of these assumptions are difficult to meet in policymaking and policy implementation contexts.

Design thinking's nonlinear, iterative approach fosters a different pattern of decision-making. Information is "perfected" in the discovery, test, and retest cycles. Human experience becomes central to judging the value of solutions. Policy shifts from being an end product to a prototype, or hypothesis. Implementation is an equally weighted step within the whole iterative process. Further, design thinking is oriented toward outcomes. It is more of a research and development–style approach than a choice or decision point model. It is these differences with rational policymaking that offer new possibilities for education policymaking.

Centering the human experience and elevating human needs is the distinctive signature of design thinking, yet design is also unique in that it shepherds a front-end idea all the way through to a back-end product. Typical policymaking practices stop at the water's edge rather than stepping into the implementation currents. This through line from design to implementation is unusual in policymaking. Typically, an agency or group of decision-makers will design an education policy and then hand it off to educators to implement, with all its challenges and complications unresolved. The separation of policy development and implementation, particularly within government structures and agencies, is almost a given: governments have both legislative branches and executive branches. The design process challenges the assumption that policy and implementation are separate activities, "conducted by different people and organizations with different kinds of specialist knowledge and capability."[9] As a structure for decision-making and implementation, the design process offers a different ordering of roles and responsibilities that connect decisions and people across policy activities.

To be sure, a rather simple story of chair design is not a model for public policymaking. Rather, the story serves as a metaphor for a different decision-making approach, one that adapts policy to conditions, particularly to users' needs; enters the conversation through empathetic understanding at the front end and doesn't finish the conversation until the work has been prototyped, tested, and implemented at the back end; and holds the possibility for furthering social learning and with it a broadening of civic capacity to implement change. There are certainly concerns to raise regarding design thinking and its use in policymaking. Among these concerns is that privilege and power commonly rest with the designer; within design there is the power to decide with whom to do empathy work, the power to interpret the results, the power to decide the framing of the problem, and the power to pick the best solution.[10] Rearranging power relationships may be the greatest challenge in improving the policymaking process. Another concern is that the qualitative data gathered in the design process may be politically less legitimate as evidence to use when expending public dollars. In addition, insufficient attention may be given to the reality of local and national politics throughout the design process. That the positive sides of the design process show up in education policymaking is possible, but obviously not inevitable.

This chapter presents an argument for adding human-centered design activities to the education policymaking tool kit and adopting the approach as a fundamental policymaking strategy. In assigning design thinking to this role, there is the possibility of idealizing the process and what the model can accomplish. It is not intellectually valid or practically sound to assume that a different approach can carry all hopes and dreams in aspiring to better education policy. Even an idealized version of the process would fall short. Rather than presenting an overly optimistic answer to complex policymaking questions, my intent is to suggest that design thinking is worth using and refining.

First, it is important to distinguish among terms, ideas, and claims related to multiple participatory and collaborative strategies. In the presentation that follows, I focus the discussion on the principles of human-centered design but pull from the thinking and practice regarding similar practices including codesign, coproduction, participatory design, participatory policymaking, and deliberative democracy. Second, in this chapter I suggest that the design process is a uniquely valuable process for policymaking and that it can supplement the dominance of the rational policymaking approach. There is strength in rational policymaking, but it is critical to address its weaknesses and attend to more than logical ends. Third, the fundamental challenge is presented in the opening story of the Aeron chair: design thinking evolved within the material, practical, and hands-on production of industrial design and was not purposefully built for complex democratic public policy questions that affect large populations. The design process itself needs additional design and improvement to serve the goals of policymaking.

Finally, in the discussion that follows, I am guided by the primary goal of achieving better education policy even as the moral purposes of democratic decision-making follow closely behind. The primary reason to build a new policymaking approach is to make better policy that leads to improved education. The desires to serve democracy, deepen social learning, support implementation, and generate civic capacity are secondary to the development of effective policies but central to education improvement efforts. I argue that design thinking can lead to more effective education policies and that the design process can help us reach these secondary but essential aims.

The section below presents key design processes and discusses their use in education policy. The second section considers how design thinking facilitates the secondary aims. I suggest that the complexity of education policymaking requires a problem-solving model that is able to match the variety of contemporary challenges, that design approaches more ably respond to questions of equity and democratic deliberation, and that design thinking facilitates social learning. The final section presents limitations and criticisms of design thinking before concluding with observations on implications for altering education policymaking processes.

POLICY AND DESIGN

The genius of design thinking rests in the two stages of empathy and iterative prototype testing. They bookend the more traditional brainstorming and problem-solving steps. The empathy, or discovery, stage is about listening and understanding the challenge. While it is easy to write this part of the process off as expendable, there is a very real cost to excluding people at this stage, because it is here when decisions are made about the source of the problem and the values at stake. Taking stock of problems through empathetic discovery slows the mad dash toward solutions. The final stages of prototyping and testing create meaningful feedback loops that encourage policy redesign and improvement. This section discusses the value of these two stages in more detail.

Empathetic Discovery and Problem Definition

The use of the word "empathy" in this discovery stage of design thinking may seem curious, but it is appropriate because it signals the work designers must do to understand people within the context of the design problem. Within this construction, a failure in the usefulness and effectiveness of a product can be interpreted as a failure of empathy. Even education policy breakdowns can be attributed to a failure of empathy among policymakers. In the policy arena, a failure of empathy is not about kindness or sympathy but instead is about a lack of deep understanding of the human situation within the policy context. Take, for example, a decision I worked on in 2013 as part of a policy team at the US Department of Education. Secretary Arne Duncan was reconsidering timelines for states to implement new teacher evaluation systems. Race to the Top and the No Child Left Behind (NCLB) waiver initiative required these changes, but the deadlines for implementation were again at issue. The new evaluations had proven to be complex; they had to include a measure of student growth, based on new assessments, tied to new learning standards such as the Common Core State Standards initiative. It was a heavy lift, and states were struggling. The policy question on the table was whether to maintain the previously established timelines or give states additional time to link new standards, assessments, and teacher evaluations. As a policy team, we heatedly discussed and debated options for two months before deciding to move forward with just one year of additional leeway. In the end, it was a policy decision with tremendous implications.

Rather than creating a valve to let off steam, the continued policy pressure forced the implementation of evaluation systems that were underdeveloped, untested, and mistrusted. Former Department policy adviser Chad Aldeman explains that as an administration we "wildly overestimated the field's capacity to improve teacher evaluation systems."[11] The decision to maintain the quick implementation timeline increased the growing backlash against testing and standards. As Aldeman notes, during this period the percentage of parents choosing to opt out of state tests rose sharply, and the number of states planning to use a Common Core assessment dropped by more than half in five years.[12] Just two years after our policy decision, the 2015 passage of the Elementary and Secondary Education Act eliminated federal oversight of teacher evaluation systems for the foreseeable future.

At its core, the question we had struggled to answer was whether the Department of Education should hold fast to an aggressive school accountability timetable or risk postponing implementation beyond the upcoming election cycle. A new presidential administration could choose to weaken the Obama administration's accountability agenda, which was based on the evidence that teachers were "the most important in-school factor affecting growth in student achievement."[13] The implementation timelines had already been settled in agreements with more than half of the states, and front-runners were putting the evaluations in place despite political headwinds. There were very good reasons to stick with the original deadlines.

Unfortunately for us and many school systems around the country, the question we struggled over was the wrong question. The real question of consequence at that moment was whether states could effectively and fairly implement these new policies. If the answer to that question was a resounding "no," then we had virtually no chance of achieving the desired policy outcomes.

There is plenty of room to support or critique the evaluation policy itself, but giving attention to the process shows that we did not recognize or deem important enough the real challenges of making large structural changes and tying them to people's employment decisions. Our policymaking process was intensive but limited to a couple dozen participants in a time frame of a couple of months. Department-appointed teacher ambassador fellows had heard from educators across the country in the preceding months; some voiced support for teacher evaluation systems, and some were vocal about the need to give teachers and principals more time to learn the standards before they were held accountable under them. Although the stakeholder outreach was important, the process wasn't meant to increase deliberation. The information gathered was general rather than tied directly to the specific policy proposal under consideration. And the concerns that teachers and leaders across the country expressed were downplayed in comparison to our own sense of urgency to see the policy succeed. Ultimately, the decision represented a failure of empathy.

Although I have greatly simplified our team's decision process and run it through the lens of hindsight, in essence we misunderstood conditions and tried to answer the wrong question. We sought to solve a political problem rather than a human problem. We lacked an understanding and appreciation for human constraints and how they might impact our vision for a better accountability system. Empathetic discovery, at the front end of a policy process, functions as a crucial part of gathering and weighing data. The results of the process bring different questions to the table and support different calculations of the policy trade-offs. As education writer and analyst Maria Ferguson suggests, if policymaking too often happens in a fishbowl, the process of empathetic discovery can force people out into deeper waters.[14]

Design scholar Sabine Junginger stresses that policymaking must begin with the stage of inquiry and empathy.[15] As Junginger notes, the shift to a stronger human-centered orientation means that the experience of people becomes central rather than just those problems that policymakers recognize or are able to see. It also alters the power balance from the designer to the user. The users define their own experience; it is not defined by the outsider looking in. Junginger tells the story of a city council that had hired an architecture firm to update the local community pool building; they thought local citizens weren't using the pool because the building was old and rundown. The architects reached out to the community and learned that citizens weren't using the pool because the bus schedule had changed. Pool users were no longer able to travel to the pool during the same hours. City council members saw a very different problem than the one that the users experienced; council members drove cars around the city and weren't sensitive to the changed bus schedule. The real problem, says Junginger, had escaped the city council's imagination and experience.

Empathetic understanding, as an activity in the policy process, is more nuanced than standard stakeholder engagement, particularly the style of stakeholder engagement commonly conducted in response to federal and state mandates. Federal regulations often require that agencies using federal funds conduct stakeholder outreach and consultation. But under time limits and logistical pressures, mandates for greater political participation can simply become a task to check off the to-do list. This watered-down version of engagement is not meant to unearth the complexity of human experience in decision-making. For example, as the global COVID-19 pandemic continued into 2021, the American Rescue Plan Act provided about $122 billion to states to help schools reopen and sustain operations. Because stakeholder engagement is an important step, the US Department of Education included it as a requirement in the federal rules. In order to access funds, states were to submit a plan that explained how they would engage with stakeholders.[16] In less than three months, states were expected to engage with almost twenty stakeholder groups ranging from teacher associations to civil rights groups to child advocacy organizations. States were then to incorporate that input and submit a plan to the department. It was a tremendous task that made it virtually impossible for states to meet the standard of "meaningful consultation" that the department requested. Under the right conditions, stakeholder engagement can be deliberative, participative, and valuable, but mandated interactions under tight deadlines do not create the conditions needed to broaden the imagination and experience of policymakers.

By contrast, design thinking can give tremendous meaning to these activities. Design thinking offers a platform for extending stakeholder participation across multiple points in the policy process and for building broader civic understanding of policy's complexities and implementation challenges. One of the logistical hurdles to expanding participation in policymaking is the challenge of getting input on rather technical policy questions. A uniqueness of the designer's empathetic discovery stage is that it doesn't require end users to have specialized expertise but instead asks that they add their lived experience to the conversation. The traditional approach—creating and weighing policy alternatives—presupposes that participants have the technical proficiency to draft policy options and make judgments about alternatives. It also presupposes that people have the time, resources, and access necessary to engage in assessing policy details. With its emphasis on research, data, and professional knowledge, the rational decision method creates a "hierarchical ordering of expertise within the policy process" such that the public's experience is given less legitimacy than that of elites or technocrats.[17] This problem is increased by evidence-based policymaking that tends to enforce technocratic power and narrow policy choices.

Within design, the problem definition stage of the policy cycle—identifying a problem and describing it accurately—is the most consequential to the trajectory of policy, despite the fact that it requires the least technical expertise. The problem definition is based on people's experience of the situation and what they need to make the situation better. Consequently, we can consider how citizens might participate at this early stage with much less investment of time and knowledge of policy nuance. People need not be technical experts to participate in design stages. The individual investment in getting up to speed is reduced. Similarly, the later design stage of gathering feedback from prototype testing depends on the users' experience rather than their technical expertise. This reduces the burden on citizens to know policy details and political dynamics before engaging in policymaking.

Further, the design process does not require that the same people follow through the full policy cycle and participate at each step. In the example of designing a chair for the elderly, we might assume that the original work of empathetic discovery was based on the experiences of one group of people and the testing and iteration based on the experience of others. What was important to the chair designers was responding to needs and supporting the activities of people in general rather than particular individuals.[18] This allowance in design creates the possibility that federal and state policy development can incorporate the user experience at different stages of the process and among different groups of people while still meeting the end users' needs. The design allowance also opens policymaking beyond constrained geographic boundaries, and advocacy and lobbying representatives. Working with different people at different steps in the process supports the real practices of federal and state policymaking that do not typically happen within a single community, even a community that stretches across states or districts. This structural flexibility reduces barriers to participation. The design process reduces expectations of policy expertise and elevates experience as legitimate evidence for decision-making.

Design and Redesign

The natural world is filled with feedback loops. Tree leaves change color in the fall in response to shorter days. The human body regulates internal temperature and blood sugar levels through homeostatic systems. In the man-made world, on the other hand, feedback must be designed. As design experts Cliff Kuang and Robert Fabricant suggest, "There may be no greater design challenge in the twenty-first century than creating better, tighter feedback loops."[19]

A policy feedback loop is built through measuring outputs, gathering and analyzing data, and then applying those conclusions to the next policy iteration. The cumulative cycles of build, test, see, and refine are a way to accelerate learning and quicken feedback loops.[20] As one of the Aeron chair designers said, "We developed the chair through a variety of experiments because we were out to produce something that had never been produced before."[21] Likewise, each new attempt to define policy is an attempt to bring aspirational outcomes into being, to strengthen and improve what was there before or conjure something entirely new. Organizational theorist Herbert Simon described design as the human endeavor of changing actual situations into what we prefer.[22] Simon contends that in order to meet that preferred future, we must establish feedback mechanisms that help social designs adapt to changing environments. As important as the original policy design may be, the quality of the next policy and the one after that depend on the quality of the feedback loops.

In order to establish meaningful feedback mechanisms, there must be visibility (the policy itself is visible to the community) and traceability (meaning that the activity or behavior can be traced to a particular policy).[23] Establishing such mechanisms also requires effective measurement. Typically, policy evaluations measure the success or failure of a given policy against some measurable metrics. Often, an evaluation will include a short section at the end of the report describing policy implications, almost as an afterthought. There is value in this research, but it rarely supports future policy design.

Completing the feedback loop means that there are reactions to the precipitating action. That is the nature of design thinking's prototype and testing stages. Unlike the early design steps that explore root causes and build a problem definition, prototyping forces specificity of design requirements and tests the validity of the early decisions. Design expert Don Norman explains that getting the requirements right is the most difficult part of design. He also notes that requirements made in the abstract are invariably wrong.[24] Prototyping and testing are methods of making the abstract more concrete. To this end, it makes sense that in product design a prototype is expected to be small, underdeveloped, and impermanent so it can be done quickly. The prototype is a representation of the product that will be produced rather than the product itself. Unfortunately, the imperfect prototype lends itself to the design of products and services more than it does to the design of policy.

We can explore how we might create policy feedback if we again consider policy as hypothesis and purposefully build the hypothesis testing and improvement process from the beginning. As suggested in chapter 2, policy solutions may rest on a substantive evidence base, but the policy itself—the written rules, guidelines, resources, and timelines—are hypotheses about how to put that evidence into practice.

In order to test a policy hypothesis as implemented, we will need to disentangle the many elements of the policy to measure and compare their effects. Each element of a policy—goals, instrumental logic, mechanisms, and requirements—may have its own impact and thus ought to be considered and measured as a category of its own.[25] For example, we could study what timelines make the most sense. We could examine which funding mechanisms, accountability practices, and implementation supports are most effective. We could weigh the value of the requirements we place on district and schools to meet the policy goals. These policy details can be tested. Each aspect of policy can be questioned and refined in a prototype and testing process.

It is instructive to contemplate what might have happened with teacher evaluation policies if we, as Department of Education policymakers, had given state and local leaders the time and resources they needed to test and refine the nascent evaluation systems. What if an iterative process that allowed for development and change had been built into the policy? What if we had supported districts and states in working collaboratively with teachers to test and refine fair and informative evaluation systems over a year or two? If those things had indeed happened, we would have had to be prepared for the most challenging of questions: What if the prototypes themselves called into question the efficacy of using teacher evaluation as a school improvement method? What if our original problem definition was wrong? Of course, it is impossible to know the outcome of a counterfactual. A different approach may have encountered logistical challenges and political headwinds as well, albeit different ones. Still, the alternate possibilities are compelling.

COMPLEXITY, EQUITY, AND LEARNING

Design thinking is as much a philosophy as a set of actions.[26] At its best it is creative, open-minded, and collaborative, blending realistic appraisals with a drive toward innovation. Design thinking is a distinctly different approach to challenges than rational problem solving. There is a reason the design attitude has taken hold in Silicon Valley, a world center of technological innovation and entrepreneurial start-up companies. For policymakers, though, a design approach is about more than innovation, for policy need not be solely focused on innovation. It is about creating room for greater deliberation and the possibility of increased civic capacity.

In the following sections, I return to the idea that we ought to burden policymaking with greater ends, that policymaking ought to be loaded with additional demands. In our age, policymaking must respond to complex policymaking environments, racial and social equity disparities, and the need for greater civic participation and knowledge. A design process refined and developed for education policymaking has the potential to help us meet these aims.

Policy Complexity

One of the most important tales of the last century's reform efforts, as told by historian David Tyack, is the search for the "one best system." Through the process, political and education leaders sought to define and impose the single best way to deliver education in urban settings. It was an effort to establish efficient and effective schools across the country through a standardized, bureaucratized system of education.[27] Reacting to rapid industrialization and urbanization, the movement toward one best system centralized decision-making, elevated well-educated experts, and consolidated power in elite leadership. The movement expanded and modernized the public school system but also cemented social injustices and systematically failed to achieve equal educational opportunity. In Tyack's summation, the top-down imposition of education order perpetuated outworn practices and ran counter to the "pluralistic character of American society."[28]

The enactment of NCLB at the beginning of this century may represent the pinnacle of extraordinary top-down efforts to direct efficiency and quality nationally across American schools. I do not mean that since NCLB there has been an end to standardization, bureaucratization, or elite leadership; there is no question that last century's reforms are now largely institutionalized in fairly uniform practices, systems, and structures. Rather, there is increasing recognition post-NCLB that these responses are inadequate and that decentralized and diversified decision-making may better serve reform and equity goals. NCLB may have taken the one-best-system logic of the last century to its conclusion. Indeed, the Obama administration's Race to the Top and Elementary and Secondary Education Act waiver programs, and the most recent codification of national reform efforts in the Elementary and Secondary Education Act, while largely maintaining old forms, may mark a longer-term shift toward greater localism and pluralism in education improvement. This shift may lead to better answers to complex problems.

We live in an era of complexity. Complex problems are more difficult to address than complicated problems. Complex problems are human and social problems with multiple interdependent moving parts.[29] An expert doesn't know the answer, and there isn't a how-to manual that will offer a solution. Complex problems are those that hang around for years, decades even. As observers explain, building a fence is complicated, while being a good neighbor is complex.[30] In education we could say that designing a modern school building is complicated, while mitigating education inequity is complex. The difference is more than just the degree of difficulty, however. As Richard Elmore noted, "Complexity, in its most basic terms, is a function both of the number of actors and the number of transactions among actors required to accomplish a given task. Complexity stems not just from the sheer size of government but also from the interdependence of people within it."[31]

Complex problems require different problem-solving strategies. With the variety of interrelated, multifaceted elements, complex problems require at least an equal amount of variety in expertise and experience to solve.[32] This idea—that the diversity of problems must be met with a diversity of expertise and experience—draws from an understanding of how biological systems respond to their environment in order to maintain stability. This is known as the "law of requisite variety." The proposition suggests that for a system to deal successfully with the diversity of challenges its environment produces, it needs to have a repertoire of responses that is as nuanced as the problems thrown up by the environment.[33] Essentially, diversity is necessary to address complexity.

Clarence Stone makes a similar observation in a summary of lessons learned on civic capacity: the path of education development requires "an enlarged understanding, a widened perspective on what is at issue."[34] Stone describes a school reform simulation exercise in which a mixed group of people, who normally deliberate just from what they know personally, collectively listened to each other and thus were able to weigh a wider array of viewpoints. The study found that "they attributed their expansive thinking to the ideas of other panelists who brought a variety of perspectives to the table."[35] In that same tradition, Elinor Ostrom, a scholar of collective action and recipient of the Nobel Prize in Economics, argues that public governance is strengthened through the multiplicity, diversity, interdependency, and variety among governing actors and structures.[36] A more inclusive "process of governance," according to Ostrom, leads to a much broader universe of discourse regarding the collective good.[37] It is this variety of thought and opinion that may bring new and better ideas to the table.

In our elite policymaking structures today, diversity and multiplicity are hard to come by. Even the number of people involved in the actual development of problems and solutions is limited. Over the last century that number has declined as our problems have become ever more complex. Ostrom provides an example of how we shrunk the number of participants within our public policy structures through local school district consolidation.[38] In 1940, there were 117,000 public school districts managed by local school boards, and by 2010 there were just 13,500.[39] Each one of those school boards was made up of citizens from local communities who were involved in the political process as they represented interests and weighed trade-offs among policy options. Essentially, each school board provided a structure for civic engagement. Ostrom observes that school district consolidation alongside a substantial increase in the US population means that today a much smaller percentage of citizens are engaged in the political governance of education. Importantly, this observation speaks only to numbers, not diversity. Given that public policies reflect the preferences of economic elites and that people of color are underrepresented in public policy positions, these shifts have broad implications.[40]

In Ostrom's analysis, public policymaking should begin with an assumption that neither citizens nor their officials are able to analyze all situations fully but that together they can solve complex, collective action problems through trial and error.[41] There is a deliberate move away from the model of experts gathering or extracting information from the doers toward one of increasing overall solution power by working on the problem together. Complex problem solving requires the collective capacity of multiple perspectives represented by insiders and outsiders, doers and decision-makers, people who work the problem upstream and those who work downstream. The design thinking process doesn't solve the challenges of multiplicity and diversity, but it does move our decision-making closer to democratic participation and more effective policy solutions.

As an approach, policy design thinking can incorporate diversity and multiplicity. And adopting this perspective leads to a different kind of policymaking. In the last two decades, public leaders have begun to tackle challenges through more inclusive, iterative problem-solving strategies such as design thinking, improvement science, community engagement, participatory democracy, coproduction, and codesign.[42] Denmark's MindLab was established in 2002 as the first government innovation lab and set about guiding design-based processes for public problem solving in collaboration with citizens and businesses.[43] Since about 2014 the United Kingdom has championed open policymaking initiatives through the designed-oriented Policy Lab. The United States created the Lab@OPM under the Obama administration, but the bulk of design-based policy work has been taken up through nonprofit organizations, such as the Public Policy Lab. This lab partnered with the New York City Department of Education in 2013 to test innovations that would support low-income and non-English-speaking families as they selected a high school.[44] Multiple city and regional governments across the United States and globally are working to improve government services through design processes and collaborative efforts with citizens.

Equity and Policy Design

If we are to use design thinking to multiply and diversify participation and solutions, we must deliberately design the process to include these elements. As it stands, design thinking has a built-in power difference between designers and users. Although the voices of users are included, the real power is in the hands of those asking the questions and creating the designs. The design approach may be well suited to driving democratic participation, but there are still power differentials between the designers and the practitioners, the decision-makers and the end users. That said, in some quarters design thinking has evolved into a more inclusive and collaborative process that cocreates solutions with stakeholders rather than for them. In these new forms, design thinking is used to address long-standing challenges of justice and equity. In the eyes of equity-minded design practitioners, "Racism and inequality are products of design; they can be redesigned."[45]

In policymaking, this requires a reordering of power in at least two ways: first, policy designers must reconsider the power dynamics inherent in the design process itself, and second, they must cede a degree of power over influencing policy in order to develop human-centered policies. It is important to recognize that the biggest barrier to policy design thinking may be the challenge of policy professionals ceding power. Almost a century ago, the political scientist Edwin Schattschneider wrote, "The definition of the alternatives is the supreme instrument of power."[46] But when we speak of burdening policymaking with greater ends, this is part of what we are speaking to.

Proponents of democratic processes have long argued that people affected by decisions should be involved in the process of making the decisions. "What makes deliberative democracy democratic is an expansive definition of who is included in the process of deliberation."[47] In design thinking, participation stretches along a continuum from light consultation to intensive codesign and coproduction.[48] The level of consequential participation necessary to create effective policies and supportive conditions for implementation is uncertain. There are also important questions to consider about which stage of design invites participation; most examples of participatory design tend to describe participation at the front-end, information-gathering, and discovery stage rather than in decision-making. There are logistical challenges in expanding participation in the time-consuming design process and ethical questions about whether mass democracy leads to good decisions.

A new design model, labeled Equity Design or Liberatory Design, adds new beginning and end stages to the traditional discovery, ideate, prototype, and test model.[49] The goal is to call attention to the power dynamics that constrain participation and privilege some voice over others. The first stage, noticing, asks designers to identify their own beliefs and biases in relationship with end users and consider their impact on the design thinking process. As with stakeholder engagement that is shaped by often unwritten rules of what is and isn't acceptable, so designers must be aware of the formal and informal rules that shape processes and order power.[50] The final stage, reflect, asks that design teams undertake an "equity pause" to consider the impact of design activities on users and the context. Improving policy design thinking might then add a step where that reflection generates learning that then feeds future policy improvement.

The impact of policy design must be added into that final reflective stage as well. As antiracism scholar Ibram X. Kendi writes, "Every policy in every institution in every community in every nation is producing or sustaining either racial inequity or equity between racial groups."[51] Kendi poses a test for judging racist policy: "A racist policy is any measure that produces or sustains racial inequity between racial groups. An antiracist policy is any measure that produces or sustains racial equity between racial groups."[52] To be antiracist is to implement policies that create equity and justice for all people. Design thinking too emphasizes outcomes. In design there is recognition that what is accomplished is of greater consequence than what is intended. If we are to create antiracist policies, we must understand their consequences through measuring racial equity impact. Conceptually, design thinking's prototyping and testing stages lessen the guesswork and uncertain predictions that accompany policymaking and focus attention on consequences. As equity designers propose, design thinking is a technical tool for moral work.[53]

Social Learning

One of the primary features of civic capacity is social learning. Researchers have noted that a community must learn together about the problems they face to generate the shared knowledge necessary to act together.[54] Design thinking is essentially a learning process. Better ideas alone are useful but not sufficient for improving education. Critically, the empathetic activities at the beginning of the design process—discovery and definition—and the action-oriented activities at the end—prototype development and testing—are learning activities. The goal of each is to learn what is working and what isn't and then to make the product better. Prototypes become learning devices.[55]

The improvement science model, a form of design thinking, is built to facilitate learning. In their book on improvement science, Anthony Bryk and colleagues tell the story of the Gates Foundation small schools initiative as a tale of unsuccessful top-down policymaking.[56] Though not state or federal policy, the initiative was a well-funded and publicized national effort that attracted philanthropic dollars and federal education funding. The immediate goal of the initiative was to convert large impersonal high schools into smaller learning communities and to create additional small schools from scratch. Just eight years after it began, the initiative ended with disappointing results.[57] In the telling of this story, the authors particularly fault the initiative for not creating a system for the many schools to "capture their learning, refine it, and transform it into a collective force accelerating wider-scale improvements."[58] The small schools initiative changed the structure and operations of hundreds of schools across the country, yet educators within those schools were largely working on their own. The primary flaw in the initiative may not have been that small schools was a poor education reform to pursue—in fact, there was evidence suggesting its value—but rather that the education field was unable to learn to improve.

In their studies of urban school reform, Stone and colleagues assessed levels of shared understanding among civic leaders and concluded that a common understanding of the problems across groups in a city is linked to the level of civic mobilization. Likewise, deliberative democracy is about learning. Gutmann and Thompson state, "When citizens bargain and negotiate, they may learn how better to get what they want. But when they deliberate, they can expand their knowledge, including both their self-understanding and their collective understanding of what will best serve their fellow citizens."[59] Deliberation, they suggest, advances shared understanding. It is an opportunity for communities to weigh competing values and order reform priorities in an ambiguous education problem space.

Community learning within design thinking, specifically within equity-oriented design models, does not neglect the contests of politics and values but instead places these fundamental interests on the table for discussion. The political task of defining the problem isn't made nonpolitical; it is raised into political deliberation. In current hyperpartisan times, this may seem foolish and unproductive. Yet, there are examples that suggest that doubling down on democratic deliberation and community problem solving lessens rather than increases partisan division and hostility and may increase trust, respect, and movement toward the public good. In one interesting study in Northern Ireland, scholars examined interactions among Catholic and Protestant participants who were deliberating over the future of local schools.[60] Earlier government demands required changes in curriculum and possible school consolidation among a divided population with religiously segregated schools.[61] Based on a facilitated deliberation process, the study results suggest that participants can find sufficient common ground to engage in meaningful and constructive deliberation, that they emerge better informed, and that their policy attitudes change as they learn. In commenting on their work across a number of venues, scholars James Fishkin and Larry Diamond note that as people learn how others are personally affected by a policy change, their attitudes shift. "People began to see one another as human beings," Diamond said. "They got to know one another and they began to develop something that is so rare in our hyper-polarized society: empathy."[62] To end our uncivil political war, they suggest, we must institutionalize deliberative citizen engagement.

In Chicago's reform efforts, local school councils made up of school leaders, teachers, parents, and community members were formal organizational settings where ideas were shared and tested over time, and not without political contestation.[63] At the community level, the local school councils engaged the largest number of people in sustained conversations about improving schools. There were other organized settings for social learning across the city. Business leaders met in subgroups of the Civic Committee of the Commercial Club, education leaders met in the Council of Chicago Area Deans of Education, and the Consortium on Chicago School Research drew together researchers and practitioners. These institutional settings, which brought different interests and perspectives into conversation, were where diverse groups collectively learned about education challenges and then acted.

Whether reform goals in a diverse community coalesce around universally supported programs may be of less importance than creating the conditions of cooperation. In the *Power of Public Ideas*, Ronald Heifetz and Riley Sinder write that political leaders must manage a community processes of learning that includes "assessing current situations, questioning previous assumptions, learning the different points of view embodied by opposing interests, inventing frames for defining problems that take in a sufficient breadth of those interests, implementing solutions by adjusting actions and attitudes as a community, and redefining problems and solutions."[64] Each of those tasks, they point out, consists of learning.

LIMITATIONS AND CONCLUSION

When asked in a 1972 interview "What are the boundaries of Design?," Charles and Ray Eames, midcentury American designers and artists at the forefront of design in textiles, graphics, and furniture replied, "What are the boundaries of problems?"[65] While that bold statement on the power of design thinking is inspiring if not thrilling, there are limitations to applying design thinking to policymaking.

The question of power distribution, inherent in almost any policy decision-making process, has to be considered and managed, as does co-optation if the design processes are embedded in government or elite organization repertoires. In addition, multiple participants with diverse views create a new competitive landscape where the cadre of policy professionals does not hold control but is "only one knowledgeable actor among many."[66] A shift in the standard processes of control may create new responses from those for whom that control is lessened. As one observer notes, as user-centered methods emerge there must be a fundamental political commitment to participatory and democratic processes at their foundation.[67] It is not possible to institute design thinking and reap the benefits without facing the inevitable changes in power. If policymakers are going to engage in policy design, they have to accept that the power dynamics are going to change.

Further, design relies heavily on understanding human experience through qualitative analysis rather than quantitative analysis. This leaves the process open to critiques that decisions are based on "soft" research. Additionally, the tools of design are typically created for small community engagement, which may limit their range and efficacy in governance and policymaking. And in many ways, the ubiquity of human-centered design works against it, as people are apt to take a piece or two and consider that the expectations are simply fulfilled. Much of government design efforts to date have focused on the more narrow and local challenges of service delivery that aren't scaled across countries or regions.[68]

The tensions between expertise and public participation in policy design are also unresolved. In most situations, design processes maintain power in the hands of the designer. Even the inclusive design process can become an elaborate way of cloaking power under a guise of democratic appeal. A critique of former British prime minister Tony Blair's efforts to improve government practices centered on the implementation of "deliverology" that brought the user into the center of existing systems rather than redesigning systems from the perspective of the end user.[69] These redesigning government efforts refined and improved public service delivery based on users' needs, while the government institutions themselves remained mostly the same.

Design thinking is not appropriate for policy design in all cases, nor is it the single answer to every policy challenge. Nevertheless, the ideas offered here could change policymaking in crucial ways. Design thinking provides a formal human-centered, problem-solving process that can bolster civic approaches to policymaking. Civic capacity for education reform is a function of shared understanding and civic mobilization, and the tools of design thinking can increase opportunities for broad community learning as policy activities move from elite offices to more democratic and inclusive settings. Policy design thinking holds the promise of expanding social learning broadly across a community and among stakeholders, including the educators and leaders who must implement policy decisions.

CHAPTER FOUR

Putting Implementation at the Forefront

IMPLEMENTATION IS TOO OFTEN a second thought for policymakers. The gap between policymaking and policy implementation is so vast that policymakers often pay scant attention to the complexities of implementation. They send policy out into the world wrapped in hopefulness that somebody, somewhere, will figure out the difficult details. In many ways, the prevailing practice of implementing through a series of activities separate from policymaking minimizes what is at stake. As researchers have noted, the joint consideration of both policy design and policy implementation is necessary for policy execution.[1] There is little value in the very best policy without its meaningful implementation. This chapter explores how we might place implementation within the expectations of policymaking and among the primary tasks of policymakers.

As discussed in chapter 3, policy design thinking provides a unique perspective on implementation. Curiously, the word "implementation" isn't commonly used in the language of design. Instead, the focus is on prototyping and testing and iterative development. There comes a point where the product is made, but even then the development continues. In recent years, for example, the Herman Miller company updated the Aeron chair to make the material more ecologically stable and improve the seat, backrest, and levers. Design uses a consistent and ongoing cycle of development and improvement that forgoes the separation between creation and implementation. If we take this same approach into policymaking, we accept a whole and continuous process rather than separate steps done by separate groups of people. From the perspective of policy design thinking, implementation is ongoing. It is a continual process of inquiry and empathy, problem definition and deliberation, testing and feedback.

Part of the gap between policy and implementation is created by timing; a policy is developed first while implementation comes later and can take years to accomplish. Much of the gap, however, is created by separating legislative and executive functions and consequently separating the policy developers and policy implementers. Yet, early policy implementation studies recognized that implementers are policymakers.[2] Their actions shape policy, as it is in the process of implementation that they make the policy fit their context. If we acknowledge that implementers shape policy at the street level with the discretion given through implementation, we want to also consider that they ought to shape policy as it is made rather than just as it is implemented.

Moving implementation from a secondary operation to an included part of policymaking sets up a new and different mindset: implementation informs policy rather than following it. In the traditional model of implementation, whereby lawmakers provide a mandate or inducement and practitioners then respond, the process is unidirectional. While that model may be suitable for some lawmaking—court decisions, for example, are often described as being "handed down," as are education policies related to civil rights and fiscal compliance—the alternative approach recognizes that the policymaking process at times needs to be more interactive. From this perspective, implementation requires ongoing interactions in which the parties negotiate and renegotiate, or coconstruct, policy and its implementation over time.

Still, our policymaking must go further. The disconnection of development from implementation limits the lessons learned through the street-level reality of practice. It is difficult to improve written policy without clear knowledge of its weaknesses in practice. In addition, implementation ought to be partnered more directly with policy development and considered the foundation of policy learning. By more explicitly considering implementation as a learning process, we can purposefully build in ways to learn.

For example, from a learning perspective, evaluation of implementation efforts switches from the question of is the policy effective to the question of how the policy as expressed through implementation can be more effective in reaching the policy aims. Finding answers requires us to embed improvement and learning in the policy itself.

In policymaking, implementation may be the best source for social learning. It is an unaddressed challenge for policymakers to design policy for its eventual improvement. Writing almost forty years ago, Clarence Stone observed, "The implementation challenge is not that of faithfully and efficiently executing enacted policies, but that of increasing our understanding of the depth and complexity of policy issues."[3] As Stone and colleagues advance more recently, civic capacity is social mobilization within a shared understanding of the problem.[4] The ability to create a lasting coalition around education reform is a product of social learning. What does this perspective then mean for how policymakers craft education policy? It means that along with developing more collaborative policy processes, policymakers must develop structures that support understanding and social learning.[5]

Policies must contain a theory of learning that expresses how learning and development will take place. And alongside that theory, policies must provide for a supportive learning infrastructure.

There are any number of ways to consider implementation at the front end of policymaking. Ground-up or ground-centric policymaking understands the conditions at the ground level and builds policy from what it looks like in practice. Collaborative policymaking is about policymakers and implementers working together on the policy development. Trial-and-error policymaking is akin to the prototyping and testing design stages and assumes a continuous improvement approach. Anticipatory policymaking attempts to foresee implementation challenges and address them ahead of time. Each of these approaches place implementation within the actions of policymaking and are considered in more detail in the following pages.

Deliberately considering implementation isn't a magic wand that can be waved to solve policy problems. Even the most careful and insightful planning is unlikely to meet the demands of an unknowable future. Yet, attending to implementation within the policy itself can create conditions that improve and smooth those practices. We can think of implementation as a process that hastens policy learning and improvement as well as on-the-ground learning and improvement. There is untapped potential in putting implementation at the forefront of policymaking.

PLACING IMPLEMENTATION AT THE FOREFRONT

It must be noted that policymaking has evolved over the last two decades. Whether it shows up in collaborative approaches that purposely diversify participation, as anticipatory approaches that foresee implementation barriers before they are reached or in the trial-and-error approach of design thinking, each assumes that implementation must be considered in the up-front design of policy. The new approaches switch perspective from the idea that failed policy is a result of bad implementation, to the idea that failed implementation can be a result of bad policy. Consequently, the quality of the process itself is an aim. This section describes four different approaches: ground-centric policymaking, collaborative policymaking, trial-and-error policymaking, and anticipatory policymaking. These aren't completely new innovations, but they embody concepts that are at the forefront of rethinking implementation within policy.

Ground-Centric Policymaking

The call for ground-up policymaking has long been a response to bureaucratic top-down policymaking. Ground-up perspectives offer a view of the experience of education in schools and classrooms, the view that policymakers can lose track of easily. However, one of the ideas I raise in this book is that positioning policymaking in the top-down/ground-up dichotomy may constrict our policy choices. There is an old truth that where you stand is where you sit. That is an idea that Richard Elmore shares in his explanation of backward mapping, which assumes that policymakers can understand implementation at the ground level.[6] Backward mapping is the process of identifying the behaviors and conditions needed at the ground level to affect necessary change, working back up the chain of implementing agencies and asking what resources are needed by those institutions to affect change, and then directing resources in that direction. The process begins at the point of implementation rather than with the intent of the policymaker.[7]

The simple idea of backward mapping captures the importance of ground-up policymaking. Yet, Elmore's analysis suggests an even more critical idea that might be called ground-centric policymaking. As he points out, policymakers often imagine policy change as altering the systems nearest to the policymakers rather than nearest to the practitioners. This has the effect of changing administrative systems rather than systems of teaching and learning. The real value to backward mapping, Elmore argues, is that the method directs attention to supporting change at the point of action, at the delivery level within schools and classrooms. We simplify the notion too much in calling it ground-up. Elmore's approach suggests that the smart policymaker asks early in the discussion, "Can you tell me what this looks like in practice?"[8] This act places the activities and interpretations of those closest to the problems at the center.

For example, I worked with a team at the US Department of Education to rewrite regulations for the Comprehensive Centers program, a group of regional centers that provide technical assistance to states to implement the provisions of federal law. The Department of Education enlists research and support organizations to provide a range of services to states without charge. It seems to be a great setup, as states receive free expert support tailored to their individual needs. Yet one of the long-running challenges with the program is that state agencies, which have little or no bandwidth to manage anything other than their current responsibilities, are asked to manage the multitude of administrative details needed to actually receive the support. Some people describe this through analogy as the challenge of the "free puppy." The puppy may be given freely at the outset, but the ongoing care and upkeep are costly. If the Comprehensive Centers program were to take a ground-centric approach, it might start at the point of ground-level collaboration and involve state agencies in determining what the program currently looks like in practice and the resources necessary to take advantage of the expert services on offer. The policy may then be written to provide the resources necessary to states and districts to access the services.

Policymaking has to make sense at the delivery level to make sense at the top of the system. This is harder than it looks. Under Prime Minister Tony Blair, the United Kingdom restructured government in an effort to personalize and improve government service delivery. It was an approach to service delivery labeled "deliverology." While deliverology focused on implementation, it centered change in the routines of administrative units, the units closest to policymakers. As critics have noted, it "should have meant that services were re-conceived from the perspective of the end user rather than the architecture of the system," when in reality it often meant "wrapping the same menu of services around them in a different way."[9]

Designing policy that is ground-centric can, in actuality, be done through either a top-down or bottom-up style. The key in either direction is to identify where in the system, according to Elmore, to delegate discretion over decision-making. The role of the policymaker is to make that identification and deliver resources and organizational structure to support success. With discretion at the ground-level, learning happens at the points closest to delivery rather than just among policymakers.

Collaborative Policymaking

Collaborative actions of policymaking including the codesign, coproduction, and coevaluation of policy were introduced in chapter 3. There are any number of arguments to support collaborative approaches to policymaking, among them that many minds are better at solving problems than fewer minds, that multiplicity and diversity are needed to match the complexity of social problems, and that democracy is premised on the value of democratic contribution. From the perspective of civic capacity, the community must together draw lessons from past implementation to solve future problems. Noncollaboration is problematic not just because it reduces the size of the groups that create policy but also because it decreases the size of the groups who learn about policymaking and the conditions necessary for success.

Noncollaboration is especially problematic for educational governance. Not only do policymakers lack local knowledge, but implementation is also often undermined by a failure to align problems, solutions, actors and resources with the conditions on the ground.[10] By contrast, deliberative collaborative efforts can bring forth needed knowledge, stimulate mutual learning, and build joint ownership over solutions.[11]

The research-practice partnership (RPP) is a model of intentional collaboration present in school systems across the United States. RPPs are locally based collaborations that establish working relationships between school district leaders and university-based and nonprofit-based researchers. Early RPPs were revolutionary in that they harnessed the expertise of local researchers to conduct research with school district data that addressed school districts' needs, not just academic needs. RPPs are not broad civic structures but are representative of the type of problem solving that can happen within partnerships among community organizations. The useful back-and-forth engagement among practitioners and researchers is what distinguishes an RPP from traditional researcher-as-consultant models.

The Chicago Consortium on School Research set the pattern for influential RPPs. In the late 1990s, researchers found that course failure and attendance in the ninth grade predicted eventual high school graduation.[12] Based on this and succeeding research, the school district adopted an "on-track" indicator as a measure of high school performance. Yet, the early results were not as hoped. School principals reported they did not have the information necessary to develop interventions and monitor their success. It was not until researchers worked more collaboratively with educators that they were able to make the research useful. The proximity among researchers and educators and between policymakers and educators is a factor in policy collaboration. A collaborative policymaking model includes upstream and downstream actors in the policy process and calls for civic arenas that facilitate knowledge sharing, sustained dialogue, and mutual learning.[13] Today, the high school graduation on-track indicator is used in schools across the country.

Currently, the US Department of Education uses collaborative policymaking in its negotiated rulemaking, nicknamed "neg-reg" for the negotiation of regulations, or rules. Under negotiated rulemaking, an agency brings together a committee of stakeholders to negotiate a proposed rule before proposing that rule publicly. The objective is to involve stakeholders early in the process, identify the information and data necessary to resolve issues, and gain consensus on the new rule or parts of the rule, all with the aim to increase buy-in from stakeholders and ease the process of implementation.[14] Under the Higher Education Act, the secretary of education is required to use negotiated rulemaking in specific circumstances. If a committee representing stakeholders is able to come to consensus on a proposed rule, the department will use the consensus language in its proposed rule and expect that committee members will refrain from commenting negatively on that language. Both sides see a win in the process. As scholars note, the "up-front investment in effective collaboration can sometimes save considerable time and energy in downstream implementation. Once stakeholders achieve a working consensus, the literature suggests that implementation can occur quite rapidly."[15]

There are limitations to the process. It is used in a narrow set of fairly technical policy cases, such as higher education accreditation, where there is an identifiable group of stakeholders representing interested parties. Still, it is an act of policy coproduction. For example, the department recently held neg-reg sessions regarding higher education accountability. There is broad concern that students invest time and resources in occupational training but that their earnings are not sufficient to afford repayment of that debt.[16] Critics argue that higher education often promises more than it delivers. From the federal perspective, there is an expectation that students are able to obtain "gainful employment" after completing career preparation programs. The department wants educational institutions that receive federal funds, including student loan support, to provide programs that lead to sufficiently remunerative employment. Attempts to negotiate a new policy that would protect students underwent the neg-reg process. In this instance, one negotiator stood out from others on this issue, and the group was unable to reach consensus. Yet, the collaborative process was in place. There is precedent in federal rulemaking for collaborative actions to create agency rules.

If our processes of policy development are meant not just to produce good policy but also to ensure implementation, we have to look to collaborative actions in policymaking. Coproduction creates opportunities to define the problem from multiple points of view, explore alternative policy designs, and learn within a community about supportive implementation conditions.

Collaboration is not without conflict, and it is difficult to learn collaboratively under conditions of conflict and extreme partisanship. In an unusual statement about deliberation in a polarized and uncivil world, an international group of democracy scholars recently joined together to make the case that "deliberation can overcome polarization."[17] They find that under structured conditions of deliberation, people tend to represent their own views rather than those of a tribe and, importantly, become less extreme. They acknowledge that adding deliberative elements may slow down the process of decision-making but may also generate smart, sustainable solutions and creative answers to political impasse.

Trial-and-Error Policymaking

Experimentation is a purposeful learning process of testing ideas and learning from successes and mistakes. Despite the need for innovation, we rarely view education policymaking as experimentation. Nor do we enter the process with the expectation that implementation builds knowledge to be used in the next iteration of policy. Experimentation in education is complicated in that we are rightly hesitant to extend the notion of experimentation to schooling children. Yet, if we see implementation variation and adaptation as normal and valuable, we can build into policy a process of learning. It really is a radical shift in perspective that incorporates within policy design the inventiveness of the people who deliver the services.[18] By limiting ground-level discretion and dismissing variation as error, we reduce learning. The effect is to "reduce reliance on knowledge and skill at the delivery level and increase reliance on abstract, standardized solutions."[19]

By way of illustration, we can look at the policy case of No Child Left Behind waivers as a missed opportunity to learn from a multistate experiment. The waiver policy lifted legal restrictions in exchange for state-developed plans that met specific expectations regarding academic standards and teacher evaluation, for example. The final plans were determined through a process of bargaining and negotiation between the federal department and state agencies. Over time, forty-five states and the District of Columbia were given waivers to institute their own versions of school accountability and teacher effectiveness. Applications were peer-reviewed to ensure that policies and implementation plans were held within "guardrails" regarding equity and civil rights, in particular. Yet, it was a lost opportunity for policy learning. The initiative was not designed to purposefully learn from state policy variation in the areas where states were given discretion over decisions. It was not designed to learn which aspects of the policy were difficult to implement, required greater and lesser adaptation, or necessitated additional resources such as capacity building and extended time frames. To have set up the policy to accomplish these aims would have required an intention to do so from the beginning as well as the creation of a learning infrastructure to capture and understand variation across states.

One of the upsides of experimentation is that it ratchets down expectations about making the right choices. Predicting future outcomes is a difficult business, yet prototypes and testing, trial-and-error cycles, and experiments create a working knowledge about future possibilities. Elementary and Secondary Education Act (ESEA) waiver policy development was an opportunity, then, to learn from variation under conditions that maintained high-quality provisions of teaching and learning and protected rights.

Anticipatory Policymaking

Anticipatory policymaking is the practical idea that we can address future challenges through policy. It is more unusual than it would at first appear. The COVID-19 pandemic offers an example; for years scientists have predicted a devastating global pandemic, as have writers and filmmakers, yet our systems weren't ready to respond effectively to the swift-moving virus.[20] The rise of artificial intelligence (AI) and its uncertain impact on K–12 teaching and learning provide another opportunity to address future challenges through policy. Educators are concerned that AI will have a negative impact on teaching and learning in the next few years while acknowledging that the ultimate effects are completely up in the air at this point;[21] so are the best policies to respond to the use of AI in education. As with addressing AI, anticipatory approaches require an uncommon level of foresight, imagination, and proactive decisions.

Anticipatory actions in implementation can mean either that we preaddress challenges or complexities that are likely to emerge through implementation or that we look ahead to shape the future, not just react to it.[22] Policymakers can take the first approach and design policy to address previously identified implementation barriers, much like a checklist is used to prevent errors in an operating room. Education implementation research can guide the creation of useful checklists. Anticipating needs then becomes much like developing a detailed theory of action or logic model for implementation that would detail the activities within the black box commonly left unexplained in logic models. Another method that can preaddress implementation challenges within policy is that of building in allowances or some "elbow room" that offers policymakers and practitioners opportunities for "mutual adaptation," or the ability of a project and an institution to adapt to each other.[23]

The second anticipatory approach depends less on prediction than vision. This approach imagines an open future and suggests a policy approach that is "evolved rather than informed," thus placing direct emphasis on experimentation.[24] It is an idea that is aspirational and abstract, perhaps idealistic as well. Still, it is an approach that is in alignment with design thinking in the active exploration of options. The approach connects as well with implementation research that suggests that variability can be an advantage in providing ideas for improving programs and a knowledge base for good practice.[25] Variability is generated as well through the elbow room that policymakers create. Capitalizing on evolving policy and variability requires well-formed learning structures that capture and share experience and research openly and broadly. This also requires policy structures that can determine the difference between noncompliance that reduces education improvement and that which leads to growth and learning.

There are additional challenges in this approach. There are limits to preplanning, particularly central planning, around what works where and for whom. To preaddress multiple possible future scenarios seems a fool's errand. There are tremendous political barriers to making anticipatory policymaking work as well. The process can require that government leaders take on an atypical level of risk in allowing a multiplicity of responses to flourish. The enterprise requires governments to build capacity to cope with uncertainty and instability inherent to complex problems in complex systems.

BUILDING A LEARNING SYSTEM

Implementation studies that followed the progress of the ESEA of 1965 set our early understanding of how difficult it is to create effective education policy in a fragmented education system. As a scholar of education policy implementation, Meredith Honig describes the waves of implementation research that examined how implementation unfolds.[26] Early studies evaluated what worked, looking for evidence of delivery of services as planned and fidelity to policy designs and found little success. This was attributed to a lack of will and skill (or capacity) among implementers. Other studies, such as the important RAND Change Agent Study, looked at the process of implementation more directly and documented the variation implicit in policy implementation in different places and among different people. The study noted the importance of contextual features and how street-level actors struggled with policy demands in complex, real-world settings.

Contemporary implementation studies look at where implementation works and doesn't work and why. They seek to learn about enabling conditions from examining this variation. Researchers also study how individuals and groups interpret and make sense of policy in a learning process.[27] Sense making is the process by which people come to understand their practice and how they change their beliefs and attitudes through the process of learning. Studies in this vein examined the conditions under which such change is possible. Other studies note that opportunities for policymakers and implementers to learn about policy problems, policy designs, and implementation progress can shape how implementation unfolds.[28] As the policy scholar Giandomencio Majone argued, learning about implementation and what ought to be improved is more important than policy design.[29]

In general, there are two types of learning that must happen for effective policymaking: the implementers must learn how to make sense of the policy within their particular context, and the policymakers, meaning the community that supplies policy ideas, must learn how to improve the policy over time. Previous sections in this chapter discuss how we might bring implementation to the forefront of policymaking. This section looks at how we might raise our conception of implementation as the source of policy learning and imbue it with the power to improve policymaking. Implementation is the machine of policy learning.

John Dewey characterized democracy as the use of social intelligence to solve social problems.[30] Social learning that aids policymaking is about more than gathering information; it is also about the weighing of values, beliefs, and interests and the deliberately democratic conversation that brings ideas to the fore for public consideration. Dewey's model was built on the notion that policies are working hypotheses. It is an experimentalist model that relies on learning from implementation. There is a stark difference between viewing policy as complete at enactment and seeing it as a hypothesis that doesn't become "real" until implemented and improved.

Dewey's perspective on learning by doing allows us to see variation as productive. The variability of implementation at the ground level becomes a source of learning, and that depth of understanding increases knowledge of implementation.[31] They are the lessons that lead to know-*how*, the knowledge that comes from practice and is the basis of policy.[32] This is the "situated knowledge" that practitioners draw from different experiences of problems and policies, the evidence of experience important to creating solutions.[33] Practice-built know-*how* accompanies knowing *that*, the accumulation of information and understanding of theory. If we recognize that implementation is a learning process that teaches what a policy really means, then we must engage a collaborative in the understanding and future policy development.[34] Collaborative practices are a means of pooling information and know-*how*.

The diffusion of ideas happens through people talking to people. It is in conversation with others that the value of "slow ideas" spread innovation and create social change. "Every change requires effort, and the decision to make that effort is a social process[;] . . . human interaction is the key force in overcoming resistance and speeding change."[35] In studies of the use of research knowledge in district decision-making, Cynthia Coburn and colleagues found that "teachers are more likely to engage with new information in ways that cause them to question their assumptions when they engage with information in social interactions."[36] Research into how we make sense of the world, sense making, describes it as an active process of interpretation that happens as we bring new ideas together with the old in a social context.[37]

The uniqueness of a social basis for learning is that it places learning in community and suggests that we can't solve collective problems without collective knowledge. Community may be defined by the boundaries of a school or district or include a more expansive notion of a community of citizens, educators, and government engaged in these problems and solutions. Street-level understanding is critical to these ideas. "The ability of collective decision-making to take advantage of citizens' situated knowledge—the fact that citizens from different walks of life have different experiences of problems and policies of public interest, experiences that have evidential import for devising and evaluating solutions."[38] It is also critical for spreading and diffusing ideas and solutions across multiple sites.

In a study that questioned why some reforms succeed, David Cohen and Jal Mehta identified conditions of success, or conditions for implementation of success. They found that successful system-wide reforms met the needs that teachers actually had, mobilized community support, were consistent with community values, and provided the necessary infrastructure of materials and training to support implementation.[39] Successful reforms combined the development of shared understanding and implementation infrastructure. A policy learning structure would include feedback loops, extended time frames, deliberative forums, learning networks, collaborative and anticipatory policymaking processes, and other supportive strategies.

A LEARNING INFRASTRUCTURE

In 1949, thirteen smokejumpers were killed in the Mann Gulch fire disaster. The story was told by Norman Maclean in his book *Young Men and Fire* and was analyzed by organizational theorist Karl Weick.[40] The smokejumpers had been dispatched to fight a Montana wildfire and in just ninety minutes were overtaken by the fast-moving flames. In his analysis, Weick describes the small team as an organization that was unable to make sense of the world it was suddenly thrown into. He noted that, in general, "people, including those that are smokejumpers, act as if events cohere in time and space and that change unfolds in an orderly manner." Yet, the conditions in Mann Gulch did not follow the patterns the smokejumpers expected. As the fire threatened much more quickly than expected, the firefighters lost what structure they had in their small organization, and their ability to make sense of events collapsed. They had neither the time nor the organizational structure to figure out how to escape. Just three firefighters survived. The events in the story are dramatic and a long way from education policy implementation, but the lessons on the interaction between social structures and sense making suggests that organizations and systems are critical to the ongoing construction of meaning and action. As Weick explains, organizations help us construct meaning and order in an ill-defined and complex world. Without time, the loss of organization meant that another avenue to make sense of the fire was lost as well. As individuals, the firefighters weren't able to understand what was happening.

If we consider implementation as the machine of policy learning, we must build the machinery, or infrastructure, of learning. In education, infrastructure is typically described as the organizational structures, roles, and resources that support instruction. In addition to expertise and knowledge, these resources include networks and social organization as well as time and materials.[41] For learning in policy, these same resources and others are valuable. There are multiple ways to establish a policy learning structure. I highlight three that are worth attention: feedback loops capture and contextualize information, extended time frames support meaningful evaluation and learning, and deliberative forums and networked communities build shared knowledge.

Feedback Loops

Education has a feedback problem. The enterprise of teaching and learning does not lend itself to quick, useful feedback. Assessments help teachers understand levels of student learning on discrete tasks, but it is difficult to measure the more general outcome of classroom, school, and district policies. Even education evaluations that determine whether a program worked as intended are rarely able to inform future policy changes. When I worked with the team on new rules for the Comprehensive Centers program, described earlier, we had an evaluation of the program in hand. The evaluation had just been completed and provided measures of program variation and effectiveness. The challenge was that is provided little useful guidance on how to improve the policy. The most useful information came from the informal observations the researchers shared in conversation rather than what was documented in the report. The research was well done, but its purpose was different than the policymakers' purpose.

A feedback loop provides information that stabilizes or alters behavior. Positive feedback can drive consistent behavior, while negative feedback can cause change. Feedback loops have to be purposefully designed. As veteran designers explain, all design stems from making sure a user knows what's going on and can figure out what to do.[42] The user of a product or policy needs to know that pushing a particular button creates a particular response. Feedback loops also need to be transparent. This perspective hasn't yet made its way into education policy design. Currently, federal programs might have a budget set-aside to conduct program evaluation, but as researchers and policymakers know, the information gathered rarely returns to those who need to figure out what to do next. In order to create better policy, policymakers and practitioners have to design better feedback loops.

Extended Time Frames

An extended time frame for education policy implementation is key. A limited time frame, the amount of time commonly given to federal and state education policies, neglects the severity of the initial problems and the possibility to learn through doing.[43] Short time frames and short-term results lead to conclusions that programs are ineffective. A number of researchers suggest that a decade is just about the right amount of time in an implementation context "where responsibilities and powers are shared among federal, state, and local agencies"[44] and in order to "avoid premature conclusions concerning a program's effects and to permit some appreciation of the extent of policy-oriented learning."[45] System theorists suggest that it just takes time for information to accumulate and flow through systems. The systems thinker Donella Meadows wrote, "If you have a sense of the rates of change . . . you don't expect things to happen faster than they happen. You don't give up too soon."[46]

There are two overall reasons to take the long view on policymaking. The first is that impacts are difficult to measure within the first years of implementation. Research on the long-term outcomes of children in the Perry Preschool Project and the Carolina Abecedarian Project provide very clear examples.[47] Although academic gains faded over time, investments in high-quality early childhood education paid later dividends by positively affecting incarceration rates, teen pregnancy, average education level, average income, and other outcomes. Studies followed preschool students as they aged into their twenties and thirties to measures these effects. Similarly, a later look at the impact of the Moving to Opportunity experiment of the 1990s that allowed families to move from high-poverty housing projects to lower-poverty neighborhoods captured the effects on younger children who had time to grow older.[48] The new study found that Moving to Opportunity significantly improved college attendance rates and earnings for the children who were young when their families moved. The program ended with uncertain results when measured on a short time frame; now, federal legislation may take it up again. The evaluation shows that steady persistence and improvement would have paid off from the get-go.

The second reason is that short time frames limit the possibility of learning by doing.[49] For example, evaluation studies in the early years after passage of the ESEA in 1965 found that disadvantaged students showed little basic skills improvement. After a decade of implementation studies, however, researchers noted substantial improvements in education performance. These later studies noted that "there was a pattern of learning by program administrators and their congressional supporters as they identified obstacles and then devised various strategies to deal with them."[50] A recent study of Obama-era School Improvement Grants implementation looked at the long-term impact of the school turnaround models across four states.[51] The researchers found gradually increasing student achievement in elementary and middle schools during the three reform years and that second-round schools had somewhat larger effects than first-round schools. The improvement may be attributable to organizational learning over time as later schools learned from those in the first round or as state leaders learned better ways to support schools.

Finally, we must recognize that policy itself is invented in the process of implementation. This raises a challenge of ending implementation too soon. If policy isn't realized until implemented, particularly as implemented under a variety of conditions, then a typical policy timeline of a few years curtails learning what was there in the policy in the first place. Short time frames mean that policymakers are making decisions on even more imperfect information than realized. Extended implementation time frames support learning and improvement.

Deliberative Forums and Improvement Communities

Collaborative policymaking calls for the creation of forums for knowledge sharing, sustained dialogue, and mutual learning among upstream and downstream actors, those in policymaking positions, and those in implementing positions.[52] Modern deliberative forums revive old ideas of townhall-style democracy where the public discusses and debates public issues. Democratic deliberation, as is the case with social learning and sense making, calls on a collective intelligence or a collective wisdom that grows from learning over time and learning from mistakes and leads to smarter decisions.[53] This collective wisdom is a product of both a diversity of intelligence and perspectives as well as the new ideas that emerge through group process. Even when addressing technically complex problems, experiments show that "average citizens can, under the right conditions, collectively produce smart contributions and proposals even on extremely technical debates."[54]

Today, deliberative arenas are described as minipublics, citizen juries, consensus conferences, and citizen assemblies. They are each different approaches to organizing public debate but share with the townhall a more individual scale of interaction and a focus on effective engagement and deliberation.[55] The goal of the deliberative process is to create spaces where people are motivated to weigh competing arguments and arrive at considered judgments. In the estimation of deliberative democracy scholars, public discussion clarifies "the will of the people" and supports learning.

Another example of a deliberative design approach is represented by networked improvement communities in the improvement science tradition. Education improvement science, furthered in the work of Tony Bryk and colleagues at the Carnegie Foundation, is based on design concepts: problem-centered, user-centered, and iterative. Yet, the process is structured within formal, intentionally designed communities that work together over time to tackle challenges through collective action.[56] Networked improvement community organization solves some logistical problems by creating localized problem-solving units. In their smaller size and constrained decision-making space, they are able to address problems over which they have direct influence or authority. The network structure also facilitates social learning across institutions and provides a support structure for ongoing implementation improvement. Yet, stable communities require organization and management and are difficult to keep operating over time as people, priorities, and funding change. The infrastructure needed to keep a community together may be more suitable for localized decision-making rather than federal- or state-level work.

The future of education policymaking must incorporate ground-centric, cooperative, anticipatory, and trial-and-error–style processes and build a learning infrastructure to support these practices. To get to this, we must deliberately create a learning and feedback infrastructure, perhaps through government set-asides that purposely build the necessary supports for policy implementation and learning. The expanded goal of policymaking becomes that of creating policy that can be implemented well, not just policy that is implementable but rather policy that shrinks the gap between policy and implementation, that creates avenues for iterative improvement, and builds the sum total of our know-*how*, or process knowledge, along with our know-*that*, or content knowledge.

CONCLUSION

"Every boat is copied from another boat," wrote the philosopher Emile Chartier. "It is clear that a very badly made boat will end up at the bottom after one or two voyages, and thus never be copied. One could then say, with complete rigor, that it is the sea herself who fashions the boats, choosing those which function and destroying the others."[57] Likewise, it is implementation that fashions policy.

Generally, policymakers tend to build the boat anew each time and not learn the lessons of boatbuilding based on what the sea sends back. There is more to this than the notion of natural selection and the useful idea that the practice of policy experimentation and testing will offer new improvements that can be copied. There is also the Deweyan connection of knowing and doing, that knowledge is not just handed down as an abstract lesson; rather, "knowledge is a by-product of activity: people do things in the world, and the doing results in learning something, that if deemed useful, gets carried along into the next activity."[58]

In the last couple of decades, new forms of governance based on similar ideas have developed alongside these changed policymaking norms. The new governance models are a response to complex social problems. In attempts to address high levels of uncertainty, governments in these new forms draw on innovation, experimentation, and collaborative decision-making. They emphasize participation and deliberation from across society—government, the private sector, and the community—to determine what is of public value, whereas older styles looked to political and policy experts to define the public interest.[59] New governance takes both a pragmatic and democratic turn in managing complexity, encapsulating a Deweyan approach to government and education that relies on real-world experience and trial-and-error improvement.[60] The new norms for policymaking follow suit. Placing implementation at the forefront—attending to the form and practice of implementation in the early steps of policy design—brings implementation into the larger understanding of policymaking affirmed through the arguments in this book: that policymaking ought to deepen democracy, civic capacity, and social learning even while it achieves improved outcomes.

Placing implementation issues at the front end of policymaking will require that we rethink our current vision of policymaking. We will need to attend to social learning in the policy process; build a more robust and useful policy learning infrastructure; reduce our reliance on fidelity, that is, the extent to which the policy was implemented as designed; and increase our reliance on sense making and policy guardrails in place of compliance. As explored in the next chapter, placing implementation issues at the front end of policymaking will rely to a greater extent on the nongovernmental sector as critical partners in a learning enterprise. These deliberative and collaborative processes may not be appropriate for all policy all of the time, but they must be added to the repertoire.

CHAPTER FIVE

Harnessing the Role of Policy Intermediaries

LOCAL TOWN SQUARES ACROSS the country have long been designed for public gathering. Communities create shared geographic spaces, whether as a small park or a sprawling court, for social interaction, commercial markets, and political assemblies. As democracy developed in ancient Greece, citizens purposefully structured the town square for public meeting and decision-making. The agora, or gathering place, was a delineated space generally enclosed by government buildings: civic offices, law courts, and a council house for the democratic representatives of the citizenry. The agora was a purposefully built environment that supported representative democracy and was for centuries the civic heart of Greek communities.[1]

While the Greek agora was a physical site, it had symbolic value along with its functional value. In Athens, the architectural design of the council house was square, with interior seating for the council along three sides and an open fourth side that allowed public visibility into the chamber and thus into the deliberations. As a place for public gathering and shared information, the agora signified the decentralization of power and broader public participation in civic life.[2] In addition to the physical setup, the architectural style for the council house was symbolically important. Its open entry way was flanked by Doric pillars, the oldest and simplest form of Greek columns, with fluted sides and plain round tops that were previously used only to decorate Greek temples. The Doric decoration of the council house was the first time the style of the temple sanctuary had been used on a secular building. The builders of the council house borrowed the symbols of the religious temple to characterize the space and the activities that took place within the space as distinct from daily activities. The architecture was emblematic of the new democratic political order, as it represented a new transparency and accountability, and the symbolism of religious embellishment elevated the nature of political activities.[3]

I use the agora as a metaphor for a democratically structured policy space. Today's policy spaces don't have the same physical boundaries of the ancient agora, but the modern term "policy space" similarly delineates a place within which public policies are developed and decided. Like the agora, a policy space is purposefully built by its participants to structure the activities of policymaking. The boundaries may be drawn to enclose an elite policy space or enlarged to be more broadly democratic. Either way, the policy space is shaped by its participants.

Today's policy spaces extend beyond government to include multiple civic actors and physical centers. When the Elementary and Secondary Education Act passed in 1965, there were few civil society organizations focused on developing and evaluating social policy. The group of education policy experts was so small that the act was said to have been largely written by one person. Today, there are thousands of organizations informing education policy, conducting research, and providing schools and districts with technical assistance and consulting services. A 2020 report found that there are more than 1.7 million nonprofit organizations in the United States, with over 170,000 of those designated as education nonprofits.[4] Further, over 40 percent of all nonprofits reported that public policy and advocacy are part of their organization's strategy. In total, thousands of education-related nongovernmental organizations are involved in policymaking. This tremendous increase in the number of policy-oriented organizations over the last decades creates new policy spaces in which participants express views, deliberate with each other, and effect change. A broad constellation of nongovernmental actors, specifically those in intermediary organizations—such as nonprofits, advocacy organizations, think tanks—contribute to shaping our policy spaces today.

A new approach to policymaking, with policy design thinking and implementation at the forefront, requires new democratic and design-oriented policy spaces. New policy activities, such as civic capacity, social learning, and deliberation, require new public squares. This chapter sets out a more purposeful and elevated role for intermediaries in the education policy space, that of reinvigorating policymaking from the intermediate position between decision-makers and practitioners.[5]

Nongovernmental policy intermediaries are a structural feature of the policymaking world, a substructure in political science terms, and have exploded in number over recent decades. They work in policy spaces and as creators of policy spaces. In this chapter, I argue that the manner in which they develop policy matters. It matters for the quality of policy produced, for the success of implementation, and for the mobilization and sustainability of reform. It matters because policy intermediaries can, under the right conditions, amplify diverse voices that contribute new ways of conceiving of our problems and solutions. As primary actors, nongovernmental policy intermediaries can restructure education policy spaces so as to be people-centered, deliberatively democratic, and oriented toward social learning and civic capacity.

The ask of education policy intermediaries is that they take on the burdens of supporting a deliberative process. As policymakers, they do not simply suggest solutions or inform policymakers about certain issues. They create distinctive practices of public deliberation that help us determine where the public interest lies and what our common obligations are.[6] This grander expectation evolves from the requirements of policy design thinking and deliberately democratic policy development. It is an expectation for policy intermediaries to use their expertise to not just suggest policy improvements but also manage deliberative design processes.

There are cautions to raise while championing this approach. Among them is the recognition that enlarging the role of intermediary organizations is a substitute for neither democratic participation nor for democratic processes. We must be careful to note that public network partners are not part of representative government. These organizations can and do represent interests, values, or preferences of their own or of their funders.[7] As one political scientist suggests, governance with some of the people, cannot make up for the lack of government by and of the people.[8] In other words, intermediary organizations and even stakeholder and advocacy groups are not the citizenry. I will raise these and other cautions in the pages that follow even as I argue for a robust role for education policy intermediaries.

EDUCATION POLICY INTERMEDIARIES

For this discussion, I define a category of policy intermediary organizations that have three distinctive features. First, these are organizations that supply policy ideas to decision-makers within government and thus serve at times as policymakers, broadly defined. Second, these are organizations that work directly with education practitioners in supporting implementation, evaluating programs, and disseminating policies and programs. Third, they seek a "public good" outcome that represents a collective interest rather than private interests in which benefits would accrue solely to members of their organizations.[9] Policy intermediaries can take on any number of organizational forms or missions. Think tanks, advocacy organizations, research firms, consultants, associations, and technical assistance providers can all function as intermediaries, and their funding sources may include government grants, private contracts, and philanthropic support. The distinguishing features in this definition center on their actions, not their form or funding.[10]

The expectations I raise depend on the quasi–middle management intermediary role. The education scholar Meredith Honig defines intermediaries as "organizations that operate between policymakers and policy implementers to enable changes in roles and practices for both parties."[11] Hence, as Honig explains, they operate independently and offer distinct value not present in either party while mediating or managing change in both parties. The aim of designating a category of policy intermediaries is to highlight particular groups that engage in the brokering, boundary spanning, and intermediary activities necessary to enable the exchange of knowledge between implementers and policymakers and bridge the gaps between policy and practice.[12]

Bridging across the different worlds of policy and practice is no small feat. It requires an understanding of both contexts and an ability to listen to and speak to each world. A friend once explained why technical instruction manuals are so difficult to write. It is difficult to speak the language of both the layperson and the machines and programming. This is true in the policy world as well. It is difficult to bridge the gap between practitioners and policymakers. As knowledge brokers, intermediaries can facilitate the flow of information between policy and practice, bridging the gap with common language and shared understanding.

In many ways, policy intermediaries take on the activities of policy entrepreneurs; policy intermediaries advocate ideas, link policy solutions to problems, and take advantage of open policy windows. They deliberately and purposefully influence and inform policy ideas. They also establish long-term relationships with education practitioners and thus gain perspective on conditions that support or impede successful policies. As intermediaries they share resources—additional knowledge, infrastructure, and social and political ties—to both practitioners and policymakers.[13] Importantly, policy intermediaries provide an organizational link between policy and practice.

Policy Intermediaries and Design

As the number of education policy intermediaries has increased and their work with practitioners and policymakers has matured, so has their sophistication as partners and incubators of reform. In the last few years, many intermediaries have taken a turn toward design and deliberation. Policy design efforts in California, Kentucky, and Washington, D.C., provide examples.

In 2016, three California school districts and a number of stakeholders set out to redesign the primary education budgeting tool.[14] A few years before, California upended typical education funding models by shifting decision-making to local school districts. In turn, school districts now work with their communities to complete the Local Control and Accountability Plan (LCAP), a strategy and budgeting tool that guides district decision-making but is widely regarded as burdensome and unwieldy; it was once described as a "beast of a document" as it expanded to several hundred pages in some districts.[15] Rather than serving as a useful strategic planning template, LCAP development is often seen as a compliance project. In an effort to rethink how to use the LCAP, the three districts paid attention to the end users of the product, those who use the information from the district plans. This approach contrasted with the original LCAP development, which primarily reflected the views of policy-focused Sacramento stakeholders. Through a three-day design sprint, district educators and partners interviewed end users, brainstormed possible solutions, and outlined prototypes for different LCAP designs. One design team outlined a new public engagement process, another created a publicly facing report to increase accessibility, a third designed an iterative online accountability process, and a fourth group developed the fundamentals of a web-based application. The collaborative design process was possible because it was the joint project of the school districts along with five supporting nonprofit and research organizations, including Pivot Learning and American Institutes for Research.

Kentucky recently pulled together a coalition of stakeholders from across the state to develop a vision for the future of education.[16] The coalition's charge was to cocreate that vision with communities, foster local innovations, and advance policy recommendations. In a creative approach to including diverse views, about a third of the coalition members were appointed by the state office of education, another third were chosen through an open application process, and the final third were invited randomly in a process akin to jury selection. The coalition was intentionally more racially diverse than the state itself. Using a design process, the coalition gathered data through empathy interviews, surveys, and a listening tour and created a vision and a learning agenda. Now these district-based community partnerships, called Local Laboratories of Learning, are developing and testing new accountability and assessment models that will shape Kentucky education policy. Each aspect of the work is guided and supported by a policy intermediary partner, the Center for Innovation in Education. Kentucky's use of a design process was innovative, and the partnership with an intermediary was essential.

In Washington, D.C., as in most districts across the country, the COVID-19 pandemic stalled student learning and led to greater learning gaps among students. In response, the city directed more than $30 million to high-impact tutoring programs. The work among schools, tutoring providers, after-school organizations, and parents and families is led through a newly established coordinating coalition, CityTutor DC, an initiative of the CityBridge Education intermediary. In multiweek inclusive design workshops, local teams created implementation plans that integrated tutoring into complex school and staffing schedules.[17] In D.C.'s unusually decentralized governance system, the intermediary organization plays a crucial role in coordinating and supporting the coalition-driven initiative. The coalition director described the task of the intermediary as helping put structure around the policy.[18]

Across these stories there are similar themes. Each is a tale of the possibilities of design thinking as public problem solving. And each is a story of partnerships among public education agencies and nongovernmental organizations. The additional organizations were key. They provided the administrative infrastructure necessary for collaboration, the skills needed to lead a design thinking process, and additional knowledge of local history and needs. Most importantly, they each created an agora, a policy space in which to work out the problem together. The story of concerted reform efforts in Kentucky, California, and Washington, D.C., today and certainly anywhere across the country is a story of the necessity of education intermediaries.

RAISING EXPECTATIONS FOR INTERMEDIARIES

There is a long-running idea that states are the "laboratories of democracy," that they lead in developing innovative policies and programs.[19] In contrast to a staid and slow-moving federal government, it was argued that states could experiment with new policies and test their outcomes before they moved to the national stage. Yet, states have a difficult time serving as sites for the production of ideas.[20] States are restrained by inadequate budgets, limited policy expertise, and the political costs of taking risks. In their recent article "The Myth of the Laboratories of Democracy," legal scholars Charles Tyler and Heather Gerken argue that policy innovation and experimentation are the work of third-party organizations today.[21] It is the advocacy coalitions, interest groups, activists, and funders who propose solutions and drive policy experimentations. With relatively few resources, states are hindered from taking on the heavy lift of innovation. As the authors write, policy innovation "requires the expenditure of considerable time and money to determine which problems government should prioritize; what are the potential solutions to those problems; and how should those solutions be implemented in the form of specific legal rules, programs, and policies."[22] States rarely have the capacity to take on new initiatives, particularly when creating them from the get-go. Education policy intermediaries—organizations that both inform policy and work with practitioners—are key suppliers of that additional capacity in policymaking.

Capacity isn't the only reason I suggest expanding the role intermediaries play in developing policy, but it is an important one. Deliberative work and the policy design thinking processes described in the previous chapters are labor-intensive. It takes effort and time to convene communities, work collaboratively through problems, define a new vision, and then go on to prototype and test options. Policy intermediaries, with their expertise and outside perspective, provide state and local leaders with invaluable resources they wouldn't otherwise have access to. A second reason is that while there are hundreds of policy ideas floating around the education landscape, few have been fully developed and tested. There is a need for well-developed policy options at the federal and state levels. Education policymaking also needs well-formed feedback loops to inform improvements, and policy intermediaries are uniquely positioned to design and support effective feedback structures. And finally, policy innovation requires new understandings of what is and isn't reasonable in schooling. Policy intermediaries can create different arenas for policy deliberation that bring new perspectives and diverse voices to the table. These ideas are explored in greater detail in the sections that follow.

An Engine of Policymaking

A fundamental need of deliberative policymaking is system capacity to host authentic, inclusive, and consequential deliberations.[23] These activities are expensive and time-intensive, and despite its enormous size, the policymaking apparatus of the US government is relatively small. At the US Department of Education, more than one-third of staff are in non–policy-oriented roles overseeing student financial aid for college, and the majority of the rest manage congressionally mandated programs and disperse federal funds. Congress too has rather small numbers dedicated to policy development.[24] Efforts to shrink government in the 1990s succeeded within congressional offices: legislative office staff were cut, committee staff were cut, and staff in support organizations such as the Congressional Research Service and the Government Accountability Office were cut. Congress's Office of Technology Assessment, which provides research and analysis to congressional members and committees, was also closed. Staff numbers within congressional offices have grown again, but the increase has largely been in local district offices and communication roles, not in research and policymaking positions. The resulting loss of expertise and experience has reduced the capacity of federal government institutions to rethink problems and solutions and manage those actions in a public engagement process. Observers call it a congressional brain drain.[25] The policymaking process must rely on non-governmental organizations to increase legislative capacity.

I liken the work of education policy intermediaries, with their extra resources and skills as well as their links between practitioners and policy-makers, as providing a bigger engine. Policy intermediaries are in a position to drive deeper development of education policy, aspects of implementation, iterative evaluation, and, critically, design-type public engagement in policy-making. The point here is not about shrinking or enlarging the size of government; that is a different dispute. My point is about adding more experience, expertise, perspectives, opinions and civic deliberation to the process. To do that, we just straight up need more horsepower.

We also need more time. Unlike legislative and executive branch actors who work under fast-moving political deadlines, people in intermediary organizations have time. Design thinking activities are too time-consuming to be completed by decision-makers. Intermediary organizations exist in a world where time can be used in the field to ask educators and families about how policy can make things better for them. They have time to gather policy ideas from stakeholders and use that situated expertise to design and test policy options.

Well-Baked Policy Alternatives

The second consideration that drives my support for policy intermediaries is the need for more fully developed and tested policies. Policy decision-makers benefit from deeply described policy recommendations. In policy talk, people discuss how "well baked" a policy is. "Half-baked" ideas may capture attention for their newness, but unless they become well developed, vetted by friendly and not-so-friendly political and advocacy organizations, they are not ready to move forward. Inexperienced advocates learn this lesson over time. Take, for example, an experience I had at a well-regarded national advocacy organization at the beginning of a new presidential administration. We crafted a policy briefing sheet in preparation for a meeting with the newly appointed policy team at the US Department of Education. In our material and presentation, we recommended that the department take on a number of high school reform initiatives. Our policy recommendations were short enough that they were captured in a three-page handout. Years later when I had the opportunity to work on high school policy at the department, I realized how large the gap was between the aspirations of our policy recommendations and the depth and specificity needed to fully develop policy. There may be a fine line between balancing succinctness with thoroughness when communicating with busy people, but nevertheless, our ideas weren't well-baked. They were suggestions, not policies. As suggestions they could inform staff perspectives by providing big ideas for consideration but weren't nearly well developed enough for department staff to see the policy potential.

Policy recommendations tend to be broad conceptions that advocate direction but offer too little guidance on the choices within policy. They often leave blank an understanding and experience of the policy in practice and the reality of putting it into place on the ground. Policymakers constantly search for answers to problems, but far too often there is a gap between policy recommendations and the actual developed policy. That gap—which settles itself between the macrolevel work of furthering a broad idea and the microlevel of writing the technical and legal policy language—can be difficult for government to bridge on its own. That is where policy intermediaries can help translate broad ideas into concrete policy proposals.

The policy scholar Richard Elmore highlighted the importance of the midlevel work in policymaking. Policymakers must understand, he explains, "where in the complex network of organizational relationships certain tasks should be performed, what resources are necessary for their performance, and whether the performance of the task has some tangible effect on the problem that the policy is designed to solve."[26] The conundrum is that policymakers don't know what resources are necessary or where exactly in the system to solve the problem. Further, Elmore notes that "the information needed . . . is dense, specific, and situational. It is not the sort of information that can be easily understood and assimilated by people at the top of the system."[27] This, then, is a task of intermediaries. The task really is to work out the resources needed and the units that are critical to success. The answers to these questions help fill out the logic model that policymakers must have in mind as they look to affect change.

After considering all of these ideas, a reasonable person would ask what a well-baked policy looks like. First, it would have the imprint of a design process and deliberation. A well-baked policy would show a fine-grained recognition of the context in which the policy is to be implemented and the conditions necessary for success. This would mean that the policy would describe how the resources of time, money, and personnel should flow and to which agencies or entities. The policy would describe the key players and partnerships, outline the time necessary for implementation, propose useful metrics of success, and describe the capacity building and supports needed. In addition, the policy would identify the prohibitions or cautions to consider. In the financial world, banks are put through a stress test to assess their resilience to financial shocks such as global disasters and inflation. In education policymaking, solutions could be put through implementation tests to assess whether the proposed policies are responsive to real-world conditions.

New Ideas on Policy Reasonableness

At the risk of positioning policy intermediaries as the superheroes of education, there is one other aspect of their work that is important to note. Intermediaries not only can improve the technical features of policies through more deliberative process but also can facilitate discussions around what is valuable and reasonable in our policies. In their classic essay "The 'Grammar' of Schooling," education scholars David Tyack and William Tobin argue that the formal structures of education and delivery of instruction are institutionalized forces that neutralize significant change. Like the grammar of our language, the organization of instruction that places students in grades and one teacher in each classroom is so well established that innovation is often difficult and sometimes impossible. Similarly, routinized beliefs and values maintain current power distributions, determining which groups win and which groups lose within those systems. Underlying ideas of what is reasonable or unreasonable decided decades ago go unchallenged. But as Tyack and Tobin suggest, "Humans build organizations and can change them."[28] This can be done, they contend, if an intense and continual public discourse about education "becomes searching inquiry resulting in commitment to a new sense of the common good."

Policies are based on our understanding of, and agreement with, values, norms, and public ideas. There is a hope in social engagement that nonprofit organizations will be able to give voice to minority perspectives and bring innovative ideas and perspectives to public conversations. The "reach" that nonprofit organizations have into local communities "and their ability to build and maintain relationships, as well as their capacity to target 'hard to reach' groups enable them to act as advocates and niche experts who involve service users."[29]

As described in chapter 3, problems of complexity require that policy ideas must be at least as diverse as the problems we are tackling. Policy-making processes must generate ideas and proposals that are more likely to tackle the cultural and political status quo in order to make substantive change. Social scientists have found that there actually is wisdom in crowds, that "diversity trumps ability." Cognitively diverse groups outperform a collection of the best and the brightest.[30] Deliberatively democratic processes that engage diverse perspectives have the potential to separate bad information, arguments, and interpretations from good, create new solutions out of the diversity of ideas, and reshape individual views of the problems and the possibilities.[31]

Civic capacity theory advocates for creating more public arenas for addressing education reforms based on evidence that broad community coalitions are able to disrupt existing practices and create new relationships and systems that further change. Clarence Stone and colleagues contend that creating civic arenas places individuals within community-oriented roles as civic actors, and this context thus shapes their contributions.[32] This kind of policy engagement encourages movement from narrow advocacy interests to broader and more diverse representations of problems and solutions through the dynamic of deliberation.

There is an old saying that a camel is a horse designed by committee. An ungainly or ill-formed product or policy, it is said, is surely the consequence of committee work. The pieced-together quality of a policy can suggest that a central vision was lost by including a variety of opinions or responding to multiple political forces. In addition to the possibility of creating a clumsy product, committee work can be just plain frustrating. Not only must we collaborate with people of differing perspectives, but group decision-making also means that any single voice is tamped down, including one's own. At the Department of Education, for example, I worked with a team and drafted regulations for a $50 million state support program. But our version didn't last for long. It seemed that everyone within the department had an opinion about how the regulations should be written. Ultimately, there wasn't a sentence or phrase that wasn't altered from our original work. The Office of General Council made its important edits, the Office of the Deputy Secretary made its own edits, the Office of Innovation and Improvement added its take, and when the regulations seemed nearly finished, other offices with tangentially connected programs wanted to step in and edit one particular or another. It took forever to get the project done. Yet, we had to concede in the end that even with the frustration of complicated negotiations and constant editing, the regulations were better. In addition, through the process the policy changes had earned legitimacy among leaders across the Department of Education.

In public policymaking, design by committee is the point. It is in groups that we debate values and alternatives and refine our vision about what is acceptable and desirable in education. And it is in groups that we mobilize public action around those ideas.[33] Instead of exhibiting urgency or efficiency in policymaking, we may be better off developing education policies in the messy worlds of committees. The teams working to create new ways to implement California's Local Control Funding Formula were diverse groups that came together for a common goal. Rather than being design teams, they could have been called design committees. My experience and understanding of policymaking lead me to believe that we need to do more committee-type work on our way to better education policy.

POTENTIAL DOWNSIDES TO POLICY INTERMEDIARY PARTICIPATION

It is important to stress that simply elevating the role of intermediary organizations will not directly lead to democratic deliberation. Like all policy actors, intermediary organizations exist in a competitive funding environment and must sometimes structure their activities to suit funder interests. In the process, they can overlook or neglect broader issues of systemic power and inequality. Research shows that rather than being a vehicle for social change, formal organizations, dependent on external funding, quiet their radical edge in the quest for resources and respectability.[34] One observer describes this as a "tamed" sector that has largely quieted a more radical ability to force change in the governmental or market sectors.[35]

Institutionalization, professionalization, and integration into the political process tend to tame social movements and the nonprofit sector. Over time, these trends also narrow the diversity of organizations.

Diversity of perspectives may be further limited by a revolving door of personnel who transition between government and nonprofits and foundations and back again, particularly at the national level. This kind of closed circle of influence, often referred to in government as "a fishbowl," can solidify one particular way of thinking. If the same revolving set of policy actors are defining and solving policy problems, they are unlikely to question underlying conditions and challenge the ways "things have always been done." One of the hopes of building multiple deliberative forums and pushing for greater diversity in policymaking participation is that we can develop better policy by drawing on a broad range of ideas.

Scholars have also noted problems with nonprofit power stepping into situations of weak government capacity, such as in Detroit and in New Orleans after Hurricane Katrina.[36] In New Orleans, nonprofits and other nongovernmental organizations were brought in to manage a new choice-based charter school network. While assessments of the charter school outcomes have been positive, there is also a recognition that parents and families lost power to elites that led the reform effort and the charter organizations.

Another concern is that the process takes on an elite status or a proceduralism all its own. The complexity of processes and procedures becomes a barrier to entry for those who do not have the necessary expertise or the ease of access to resources, privileging some organizations over others. Further, elite nonprofit organizations can themselves mimic the technocratic elitism of government. If they are too closely aligned within the same constricted ecosystem, they can become middle-men barriers to democratic participation rather than facilitators of more broadly representative and diverse contributions.

The goal of deepening policy is a different goal than strengthening the governance hand of nonprofits. The argument for greater nonprofit participation in democratic policy development processes is not to increase the provision of public services through the nongovernmental sector but instead to enlist that sector in more constructive support for public decision-making. The expectation that the nonprofit sector takes on the burdens of more deliberative processes in developing policy does not suggest that nonprofits represent citizens in the same way that government is to be representative. While nonprofit organizations can and commonly do represent citizen interests, they are not democratic representatives with looming elections that make them directly responsive to citizen interests. They are not power-free organizations. The basic framework of government and nonprofit relations must therefore continue to assume a prominent, essential, and authoritative role for government.[37]

Oversight of education policy intermediaries rests primarily on transparency regarding funding and political activities but also transparency and communication regarding their network and their selective hiring. Policy intermediaries in education have a moral accountability as agents in the field of education that exists among shared norms and values.[38] This is also the case for new norms of policymaking and deliberatively developed policy alternatives. Accountability under new expectations of policymaking is a mutual accountability built among networked actors pursuing common projects or goals.[39]

A Note on Partisanship

I posit this need for more public participation with recognition of the hard reality of partisanship today. We live in political communities that are separated by geography and information sources. The distances between us are apparent in often ugly political disagreement amplified through social media. One of the enduring images of the pandemic era will be that of bitter school board meetings. Anger, intimidation, and threats of violence have gotten so out of hand at some board meetings that police have been called in to clear the rooms. A friend who recently joined a county school board described the contentious discussions at his first meeting as running through the night until near dawn the next morning. As one writer noted, there are issues worthy of legitimate debate—about mask wearing, school closures, and curriculum—but legitimate debate is not what's currently on offer.[40]

One of the challenges we face in a partisan and informationally complicated world is perhaps that we have too few venues for civic deliberation, too few opportunities to sort out positions, interests, and facts or find those that are common among us. School board meetings sit at the center of many political and cultural battles because they are accessible; they are local, public, and focused on questions for which most families, by virtue of being involved in public education, have a homegrown expertise.[41] At present, school board meetings may remain one of our few organized public spaces for airing private opinions and values even as the conditions created by partisanship and the pandemic limit the quality of public deliberation and social learning.

In this context, it is tempting to shorten public conversation or pull back from community engagement. However, the lesson from the ugliness of school board meetings is not less conversation but more: more widespread deliberation, more public conversation, and more understanding of policy purposes and necessary trade-offs. The ideals of deliberative democracy stress diverse participation, the norms of civility, mutual justification of decisions, and openness to persuasion. And despite political partisanship, experimentation with deliberative forums is flourishing worldwide.[42]

The design and deliberation built into an education policy development process adds to a broader deliberative system that must be built, or rebuilt, in our age. The pandemic will end, but the need for opportunities to deliberate about what is good for our children, to question our assumptions, and to revise our opinions will remain. Working our way back to civil engagement and legitimate debate will require practice. It will require more opportunities for public deliberation. Education intermediaries are key to increasing forums for public deliberation.

CONCLUSION

The potential for conflict arises when considering an increasingly empowered nonprofit sector in policymaking. Nonprofits are not representative institutions that directly convey the will of the people. They have their own interests and are accountable to funders. They can be elite institutions, lacking diversity in their opinions, perspectives, and people. All of these are serious concerns that need to be considered and, when required, addressed. My worry, however, is not that the influence of these organizations is too large but that the visions they hold of their work and our expectations of their responsibilities are too small. The primary question is not how much they participate but rather are we expecting enough from their participation.

I am suggesting that intermediary organizations should aim for larger goals: they should engage in design thinking policy development processes, their policy recommendations should reflect a responsibility for the public good, they should increase transparency around the policymaking process, and they should work toward broader and more diverse thinking by pushing against narrow and convergent thinking. Policy intermediaries can create meaningful processes that clarify the public will and create policies that represent public concerns. They can be and often are the workhorses of policy development. I am suggesting that they take this work even more seriously by understanding and acknowledging their broader impact.

CHAPTER SIX

Working Shoulder to Shoulder

New Federal-State Relationships

NEARLY EVERYTHING ABOUT the early years of education policymaking in the Obama administration was unusual. Within a month of President Barack Obama assuming office and in the midst of the Great Recession, Congress passed the American Recovery and Reinvestment Act of 2009, a recovery-oriented piece of legislation that committed nearly $100 billion to education programs. It was a flood of money that created exceptional policy opportunities. While most of the funds went directly to states and districts to stabilize local budgets and prevent job losses, the sheer enormity of funding prompted the wry observation that incoming secretary Arne Duncan was rolling in cash while his predecessor, Secretary Margaret Spellings, had been searching in desk drawers for pocket change.

The recovery-related funding spurred extensive policy development. The most notable was the $4.35 billion Race to the Top program, the largest competitive grant program in US education history. The national competition and its promise of substantial funding inspired a surge of policy changes in states across the country.[1] These unique conditions, coupled with a good deal of publicity, made Race to the Top the administration's signature policy. Yet, it may be the less well-recognized No Child Left Behind (NCLB) waivers policy, with its state-by-state negotiated agreements waiving fundamental sections of policy, that set the stage for a style of policymaking with longer-term consequences.[2]

Secretaries of education have long used congressionally granted waiver authority to amend federal rules by granting flexibility from provisions of law.[3] Over her four-year term, Secretary Spellings granted dozens of waivers to support pilot programs and reduce escalating sanctions on low-performing schools. But the Obama years were different. The era of the Obama administration was the era of the "big waiver."[4] In his first two years, Secretary Duncan granted hundreds of standard waivers, and as NCLB reauthorization languished, the secretary stepped in with a big waiver package that the Department of Education named "ESEA Flexibility," commonly called NCLB waivers. This bundle of waivers went far beyond earlier more modest tweaks to standing law. The program waived several provisions at once, offered waivers to all states, expected most states to request and receive the waivers, and was conditioned on whether a state satisfied new expectations that required substantive policy actions. Under the NCLB waiver program, states were granted eight distinct waivers from the statute in exchange for commitments to Race to the Top–style priorities including college- and career-ready learning standards, teacher and principal evaluation systems, and identification and support to low-performing schools. This use of waivers was a giant step beyond what had been done before. The policy was unusual, and importantly, so was the process.

The NCLB waiver approval process was a negotiation. States requested waivers, the US Department of Education ran the requests through peer review, and then, through an iterative and sometimes contentious back-and-forth, department staff and state leads negotiated the final terms of agreement. During my time at the department I led teams that worked with a number of states requesting NCLB waivers. Some of the state approval processes were relatively straightforward, and others led to heated arguments and delays. The negotiations were challenging, because among other expectations states had to redesign complicated school accountability systems, a complex endeavor even for the most skilled policymakers. Each state approached the task differently, a predictable outcome that nevertheless challenged the Department of Education, which is not set up to navigate individuality among states.

The wisdom or folly of the Obama administration's ESEA Flexibility policy has fueled many spirited debates, but the policy was given its ultimate comeuppance when Congress, with passage of the 2015 Every Student Succeeds Act (ESSA), reauthorized the Elementary and Secondary Education Act (ESEA). The ESSA eliminated the secretary's broad waiver authority and more, removing the ability "to mandate, direct, control, coerce, or exercise any direction" over state actions related to academic standards."[5] But despite the department's waiver authority being dramatically curtailed by Congress, there are some aspects of the ESEA Flexibility policy that are worth noting. As previously mentioned, the waiver approval process was a deliberative negotiation. During the discussions, each side had to justify its decisions with rational and substantiated evidence.

State leaders often explained that their proposal made sense for their unique education system. Armed with a detailed understanding of federal aims, state leaders could knowledgeably question the premise and requirements of certain federal policies. In response, the department had to justify that premise and its requirements. By hearing the rationale for state choices directly from state leaders, federal staff could navigate policy details and align them to larger, more common aims. Some participants would argue that referring to the process as a negotiation is too generous, as the federal actors still held a powerful upper hand. Yet, some of what happened was what ought to happen in a shoulder-to-shoulder policymaking relationship; the back-and-forth process led to iterative improvements in the details of both federal policy and the state plans.[6] Whether congenial or adversarial, federal and state leaders had to accommodate one another. On both sides of the negotiating table, we listened and learned. Unusually, policy and implementation were a connected body of work, interdependent in both theory and action.

A NEW POWER DYNAMIC

One of the challenges that gets in the way of doing business differently is a static view of federal-state power dynamics in education policy. We operate within an understanding that places federal and state governments at opposite ends of a line of power, much like competitors planted at either end of a tug-of-war rope. As one group wins, the other loses. Power gained by the federal government usurps the sovereignty and autonomy of state governments, and on the other side, power gained by states threatens federal priorities of civil rights and national academic excellence. Today, political disagreements about where that center of balance ought to rest are argued by small-government–oriented conservatives on one side and activist political progressives on the other. And there are those who see benefit in balancing to one direction or the other depending on the policies and activities pursued.

The problem with the dominance of this storyline is that it can't move us forward. The answer to improving education policy does not rest at one particular point along a continuum between centralized and decentralized power and decision-making. Even a perfect balance point does not create better policy. Yet, we set up this dynamic as a primary struggle in education policymaking. The weakness in the story is related not to its truth or fiction—there is tremendous truth in the tale—but instead to its limitations. To the extent that the NCLB waiver process worked to refine state plans and force reconsiderations of federal policy, it was through negotiated, interactive, and iterative actions. A tug-of-war does not allow for this interplay.

Though limited, the NCLB waiver process suggested a different way of developing policy. It is an almost-example that raises questions of what might be possible if we purposively built federal and state back-and-forth into our policy development. What if some policies were ultimately derived through bargaining and negotiation between federal and state agencies or, similarly, between state and district agencies? What if an enacted federal policy could be adjusted based on experiences of state or district implementation? What if the implementers, education leaders, and teachers were in on the negotiations? In picturing an idealized process, we can consider what may be gained.

In this chapter I argue for reconceptualizing federal-state policymaking and following a different federalism storyline. A new conception of federalism takes the ever-present question of what the federal role in education is and puts it aside just long enough to ask how to construct and manage interdependent federal-state relationships. My goal in forwarding this argument is not to replace state autonomy or to limit the federal role. The tug-of-war that has embodied so many education policy decisions will rightly continue; a contestation for power has value for governmental accountability and the furtherance of states as sites of innovative reform. Rather, the purpose is to add an additional approach that increases the likelihood of deliberation, social learning, and iterative improvements while placing implementation closer to the front end of policy development. If we could revisit the NCLB waiver approval process with a new shoulder-to-shoulder federalism mindset, we could create a much better process than that developed without this aim. With relational federalism in mind, we could plan for a more equitable negotiation process that gives states the power to contest and fight for what they believe is best for their circumstances. We could build structures to support learning and iterative development. We could expand the timelines under consideration to give time to testing and feedback. Like true innovators, we could have designed the process differently by considering broadened aims.

TRADITIONAL EDUCATION FEDERALISM

Education is a state and local community responsibility. At the same time, the federal government has a great deal of power and influence, especially since education is a national issue contested on the national stage. The story of traditional federal power and state autonomy reflects a standard view of education federalism as the balance of power among levels of government that emphasizes state influence over education.[7] Federal funding for public education makes up less than 10 percent of most state budgets.[8] Yet, the federal government has tremendous influence. Since the 1950s with the landmark *Brown v. Board of Education* decision on school segregation, power and authority in educational governance has shifted from local sites to state and federal governments.[9] Federal influence increased in the 1960s with the passage of the ESEA and other civil rights and antipoverty legislation. The shift from local power toward federal power reflects the change of public interest in education from a local concern to a national concern. Since the 1990s, American voters have listed education as a top-tier issue.[10] The NCLB of 2001 was the most recent high-water mark of federal expansion, as passage of the ESSA in 2015 intentionally shifted power and responsibilities to state and local agencies.

The struggle over the proper balance of federal and state power is grounded, in part, in the idea that state policymaking power is directly related to its independence from federal intrusion. The battle over adoption of the Common Core State Standards was framed as an impingement on the rights of states to decide what students should learn. A number of states altered the Common Core standards just enough to defiantly name them after their own state, asserting ownership over the end product and the process. Similarly, the headlines announcing the ESSA highlighted how states had regained independence from federal intrusion. The White House press release on the ESSA stated that the new law will "empower state and local decision-makers to develop their own strong systems . . . rather than imposing cookie-cutter federal solutions like No Child Left Behind did."[11] States commonly distance themselves from federal influence in order to assert authority and carve out autonomy over decision-making.

Yet, in the day-to-day development of policy, there is much greater integration and interdependence among levels of education governance than commonly recognized in popular discussions of federal authority and states' rights. NCLB and its 1994 predecessor, the Improving America's Schools Act, were outgrowths of state practices and were influenced by powerful governors and local education leaders. The NCLB waiver policy was influenced by state and district leaders who requested greater flexibility under the law, and many weighed in on the provisions in the final package. When President Obama announced the NCLB waiver policy, he did so with two state governors by his side and twenty-four district superintendents in the audience. The visual image of federal and state government representatives standing together, in the language of political communications, lent bipartisan support and state-level legitimacy to the new policy. The policy was ultimately created at the federal level—it was not a locally developed waiver package—but multiple local educator and advocate voices weighed in. Federal policy success is ultimately dependent on the cooperation of the lower level of government to legitimate the decisions as well as to implement the decisions. The central story of federal dominance versus state autonomy does not truly represent the interplay within education policymaking.

An important consequence of the traditional conception of federal power versus states' rights and autonomy is that it positions policymakers—and their perceptions of what is possible and desirable—within this same perspective. Policy is made within the structure of a federalism that carves out areas of autonomous discretion as the primary way to hold power over policymaking.[12] Policy is conceived, drafted, and enacted within a limited framework regarding roles and responsibilities as well as rights and authorities.

One effect is that federal education policy sets out the roles of the federal government—federal grants, technical assistance, research, monitoring—but releases federal policymakers from responsibility for implementation.

Federal policy too often assumes that the extent of federal responsibility stops at the edge of implementation, a job that is considered the responsibility of states and districts. This delineation also severs any links between policy enactment, evaluation, and reformulation—the cycle of continuous iteration and testing—for the purposes of improving policy. The distance between policy and implementation is exacerbated by the separation of federal and state policymakers in the policy process.

The challenges that play out in federal-state dynamics are mirrored within state-local interactions. The ESSA's theory of action suggests that devolving power to the states will improve education. This effort to place autonomy at the local level punted policy decision-making downstream but didn't set up better conditions for policy improvement. The distance between state policymakers and local practitioners isn't reduced. The opportunities for iterative policy improvement aren't automatically increased.

It isn't just a change of venue that is needed; instead we need to alter the layered system of policy decision-making. We need to create formal mechanisms for integration across government levels—be they federal, state, or local—that focus on social learning and continuous improvement rather than on mechanisms that establish separation and sovereignty. Prime among these is giving attention to implementation considerations at the forefront of policy development. By keeping the arguments regarding policy focused on questions of the centralization or decentralization of power, we don't get into other truly critical parts of policymaking. If we step to the side of the centralization-decentralization argument, we can step into truly critical policy actions of collaborative development, implementation, and iteration.

RELATIONAL EDUCATION FEDERALISM

In contrast to a traditional federalism model that emphasizes separation between governing institutions, a relational model looks at federal-state interactions and relationships.[13] Relational federalism emphasizes the dialogue between institutions and how institutions interact and advance policy goals.[14] Relational federalism is theorized and made practical within the legal field.[15] Scholars in this tradition question traditional federalism and argue that court decisions must consider the reality and desirability of federal-state integration and interplay. Heather Gerken, the dean of Yale

Law School, asserts that states are powerful even when working within a federal regulatory system. States don't need to be independent to assert policy influence and power. Instead, Gerken avers that "state power comes from integration and reliance, not separation and autonomy."[16] This alternate view of state power uses a paradigm that emphasizes a power to accomplish goals and shape policy rather than a power over a select set of policy decisions.[17] It is a power that is contingent on acting with others.

This perspective acknowledges that federal-state interactions are often negotiated, iterative, ongoing, and interdependent.[18] In the language of an old metaphor, this is not layer cake federalism that establishes separate spheres of governance. Nor is it a marble cake federalism that allows for state power and cooperation but is still reliant on distinctions in power and responsibilities.[19] Instead, relational federalism recognizes the power in interconnectedness: one group can't gain its goals without the other group. The aim in relational federalism is not to carve out separate terrain managed by each level of government but instead to create shared terrain.[20] It is the messy process of baking the cake together.

In order to see the power of states in a federally influential policy sphere, it is useful to revisit two framing theories that are at play in relational federal-state dynamics. The first is principal-agent theory whereby one actor makes the decision and another actor is to abide by and implement that decision. The inherent challenge is that the principal has formal authority to make policy, but the agent, who typically has greater on-the-ground information and a particular stake in the outcome, is relegated to implementing the policy. The power is being held by the decision-maker, yet it is the implementer, or the "street-level bureaucrat" in the language of the sociologist Martin Lipsky, who has substantial discretion in its execution.[21] It is important to stress that the principal-agent relationship need not be harmonious to be productive. It is the interaction—not cooperation or agreement—that creates value. The interaction can then be cooperative or competitive, dissonant or harmonious.[22] Relational federalism is not necessarily about reducing conflict but is about the value of cooperation and noncooperation in a system that mixes the two to produce governance.[23]

There are two important aspects of principal-agent theory to highlight here. First, an agents' power comes from acting on behalf of an upper level of government and thus is derived from integration within the system. The power of the agent is in implementing and interpreting the law, and thus the state as agent expands policymaking power when it is shaping and delivering federal law. To illustrate, the states that pursued NCLB waivers agreed to implement substantive and detailed federal policies. One way to see this is that they were agents who had to comply with the principal's demands. However, an alternate view suggests that states were granted additional authority and power to reform their education systems because they were implementing federal regulations. They gained additional political power to craft new systems that they determined were a better fit for their states. They were also given flexibility around established law to make those changes. States that did not apply for the waivers did not gain that extra momentum and flexibility to advance their education systems.

The second important aspect of principal-agent theory is based on a related idea that was captured in the economist Alfred Hirschman's classic book *Exit, Voice and Loyalty*. His contention is that if people are dissatisfied with organizations, they have two options: they may leave, or exit, to express their discontent, or they may use their voice within the organization to encourage change. Both are valuable levers for citizens to use to encourage education improvements. In education, we have established an infrastructure for exit through the creation of public charter schools, homeschooling, and, for some, access to private schools. In the decade leading up to 2019, the number of students attending charter schools across the country more than doubled, rising to 7 percent of public school students.[24] About 9 percent of students attend private schools. And just over 5 percent of children are homeschooled. Across the country, charter schools, homeschooling, and private schools are options for exit from traditional public schools. Less well developed in districts across the country are the infrastructure and activities to facilitate the expression of voice, particularly within the framework of loyalty. This last option represents the possibility of influencing the decision-making process from within an organization. In contrast to voicing discontent, there is an option to remain a member of the organization and participate in the process of making policy.

The power to help set policy is a different power than that expressed through exit; it is, as Gerken explains, a muscular form of voice.[25] Take again as an example the negotiations between states and the Department of Education in the process of approving NCLB waiver applications. When states first applied for the waivers, federal staff were caught off guard by the unusual variations in state plans and had to reconsider the guiding regulations. In creating new accountability systems, for example, some states designated school performance using A through F letter grades, others created measurement indices, and one proposed a system of multicolored flags to report performance. Underneath those variations were further gradations. Some states were experimenting with new indicators such as attendance, student and family engagement, dropout rates, and surveys of school culture. Additionally, a number of states reconfigured NCLB student subgroups into new "super subgroups" that had the benefit of reporting performance for more students but the risk of masking the performance of smaller subgroups, such as students with disabilities and English learners, and rendering accountability meaningless. Staff at both ends of the negotiation puzzled over how much weight should be given to each school indicator, the criterion for schools to enter and exit designation categories, the minimum number of students in subgroups required for reporting, or the expected rate of school progress. Admittedly, these are technical policy details and were negotiated within the structure set by the department. Yet, state variation won out. States had a powerful voice in shaping the agreements.

Benefits of a Relational Model

In relational federalism there is potential for improving policies and their implementation. Richard Elmore, in a classic article on implementation titled "Complexity and Control," argues that altering traditional command and control relationships and building two-way relationships increases the likelihood of policy success.[26] He likens the new arrangements to a contract between partners. Each party in the contract has a need that is fulfilled by the other party. A contract is not an instrument of coercion but instead is an instrument to determine how to get resources into the hands of those who use them, where to locate accountability, and how to create organizations that support the delivery of services. A contract is incompatible with the notion that federal power exists in control while state power resides within sovereignty and independence. That is the bargained arrangement that Gerken argues better matches what actually happens in our federal-state interactions as well as what ought to happen to influence better policy and implementation. That was essentially what we were doing at the US Department of Education with NCLB waivers. We were creating contracts with states. One review of NCLB waivers found that forty-five states, the District of Columbia, Puerto Rico, and the Bureau of Indian Affairs submitted waiver requests, revealing a preference for a negotiated, contractual relationship over the federal-heavy management under NCLB.[27]

Relational federalism recognizes the power of both the policy decision-maker and the policy implementer and the reliance each has on the other. Whether the relationship exists between federal and state actors or between state and local actors, an alternative conception of the principal-agent dynamic creates room for policy codevelopment. One great advantage is that shoulder-to-shoulder policymaking established conditions for mutual learning. New structural arrangements create opportunities for interaction and debate, and multiple institutional perspectives on a problem may produce a broader variety of potential solutions.[28]

Importantly, policy implementation stands to improve under a relational federalism model. First, seating implementers at the policymaking table raises the likelihood that implementation is considered as important as policy.[29] This moves consideration of implementation to the forefront of policy development rather than the back end. The new seating arrangements provide greater possibilities for iteration toward better policy, as they give a credible role to the implementer whose experience with success and barriers is integral to practice and thus to a reiterated policy. Scholars note that alignment of the assumptions at the core of a policy and the assumptions of the actors in charge of implementing the policy is likely to facilitate successful implementation.[30] Second, policy is edited by those who implement it.[31] From a top-down perspective, implementers are expected to comply with the policy they are given, and yet evidence confirms that policy is negotiated in the course of implementation.[32] And finally, the move away from hierarchical relationships allows for coproduction and forms of accountability within social relationships rather than solely compliance-based relationships.[33]

Setting the Right Conditions

The NCLB waiver process described in this chapter was an almost-example of what is possible, not an actual example. In many ways it was a shadow of what could be created if we intentionally relinquished the heavy hand of federal policy control and set the conditions for a relational style of interaction and policy development. Developing policy across layers of government will require that we create new ways of doing business between federal and state education agencies and also create new organizational structures of support. Rather than trying to keep federal agencies from encroaching on state terrain, we need to establish healthy interactions on shared terrain.[34] We need structures that can facilitate governing together.

First among these would be new norms for negotiation. The ground rules for federal-state bargaining in the process of policy development have to support a fair process that is beneficial for policy development.[35] States should have the opportunity to engage in the ground-level development of policy and not just the ability to tinker at the edges of already established rules. Further, the negotiation of policy implementation is ongoing, and thus the systems of interactions must continue past the point of policy enactment and across extended timelines reflective of implementation time frames.

Additionally, there must be organizational structures within agencies that are able to work across states. After the initial rounds of NCLB waiver negotiations, the US Department of Education recognized that it did not have the structures necessary to support substantial state variations in policy. Over the next years, the department worked to develop "state desks," staffed by state-level experts who were the primary touch point for state leaders and understood the intricacies of specific state systems and needs. The operational complexities of standing up such an infrastructure have been difficult, and today state desks are present but underdeveloped.

Waivers are intended to learn from variations within the rules in ways that inform future policymaking, but we are missing the necessary learning infrastructure to utilize these benefits. Federal agencies offer technical assistance to states and large-scale research activities to measure effectiveness, but the improvement and learning derived from these actions are rarely iterative and almost never inform the next iteration of policy.

Another aspect to consider is overseeing policy variations and implementation across states. Monitoring and compliance are large drivers of behavior, and among districts and schools, the consequences for not meeting federal monitoring demands are significant. States and districts care far less about a secretary's letters emanating from the US Department of Education than about the judgments of monitoring and compliance teams. But monitoring can be narrow, rule-driven, infrequent, and compliance-oriented, and efforts to control the actions of implementers undermines the agents' ability to also be responsive to context and client needs. Thus, new methods to support agents and to monitor implementation are necessary.

Different models of federalism are not without critique. One of the challenges in integrating federal and state policymaking is that it may obscure lines of authority and thus muddle transparency into areas of responsibility and thus make it harder to discern accountability.[36] And in negotiations there is the possibility that state authority could be reduced or federal overreach could be expanded (although the arguments here suggest that neither outcome would be as troublesome as often argued).[37] Still, relational federalism is not a fit for every policy question.

Relational federalism goes beyond the notion that federal policy should be drafted with input from states in that it expects policymakers to write policy outside of the old federalism paradigm and into a new paradigm that recognizes the limitations of top-down declarations. Further, relational federalism requires building in mechanisms for continual negotiation, feedback, and iteration. This will not work across the policy landscape but does lend valuable deliberation and iteration to areas of education policy complexity where the policy solutions are uncertain.

CONCLUSION

By continuing to center policy arguments around allocating power at the federal level and autonomy at the state level, we miss the chance to harness the inherent interdependence and need for cooperation necessary to produce better policy and implementation. The NCLB waivers and the negotiated process of waiver approval suggest the possibilities of a new style of partnership between federal and state governments. States have the ability to meet local needs by shaping federal initiatives, and the federal government can hold tight to national needs and the stewardship of public funds in an interactive, interdependent, and negotiated partnership.

If we desire to reap the spillover effects of increased civic capacity and deliberative democratic practices from policymaking processes, it is important to note that a relational federalism style need not stop with federal-state relationships. There is an equal need for a relational federalism all the way down to a relational localism. Hierarchical control has limits whether at the upper or lower levels of government. The ESSA granted greater authority to states to make decisions about their accountability systems, but its theory of action didn't alter the principal-agent relationship. It too runs up against constraints in the state-local dynamic that are present in traditional federalism. As observers have argued, an innovative future is incompatible with an inflexible federal policy environment.[38]

PART III

Implications of Deliberative Policymaking

CHAPTER SEVEN

A New Education Statecraft

AT THE CORE OF THIS BOOK is the argument that in order to improve education policy we must rework our policymaking practices. This chapter follows on that argument with the assertion that if we want to change the ways in which policy is made, we also need to reconsider the role of the policymaker. In two short scenarios presented below, I illustrate the contrast between current policymaking practices and the more aspirational approaches that can guide future actions and decisions.

The first scenario takes place in Washington, D.C. Education policy analysts at the US Department of Education write policy memos used by the secretary and other senior leaders to make decisions about an array of policy issues. Policy memos describe what is happening now and the problem that needs to be solved. They provide an assessment of causes, a determination of what should be happening, and recommendations of what needs to be done. Generally, memos present a handful of viable policy options laying out the pros and cons for each choice along with a tightly argued rationale behind the recommendations. Policy memos can be written quickly in a matter of days, unlike other policy determination processes that may take months to develop. In my experience working at the Department of Education, these memos were painstakingly crafted in order to get the details right. We sought out educators and other experts to understand current conditions and talked with researchers to gather data and evidence to understand the problem and shape recommendations. Each memo went through rounds of internal review and was vetted by senior leaders in a policy council before being shared with the secretary of education for his decision. Policy memos are the bread-and-butter work of analysts and represent a step in rational policymaking practices. They are also typically crafted by small teams within a particular government setting that is far from the point of the user's experience and from the places of implementation.

The second scenario takes place in Kentucky. As described in chapter 5, teams of education stakeholders are working together to design new student assessment and school accountability policies for the state and local districts. The project is built on the principles of inclusive design and cocreation between local and state stakeholders and is taking on the complicated task of creating greater alignment and coherence between state and local systems. The project also aims to shift ownership of the reforms from state leadership to local practitioners in order to support change in classroom practices and sustain the changes over time.[1] Collaborative teams are guided by policy design thinkers from the Center for Education Improvement who facilitate and manage community-driven design processes. They systematically bring in more voices to the conversation, increasing inclusion. They work through empathy-oriented processes to understand people's experiences. They work side by side in processes of cocreation. And they build internal structures to support shared learning. While improving assessment and accountability systems that will ultimately be approved by the state education agency, the policymakers are deliberately increasing civic representation in the process of creating state and local education policy. Overall, the work is facilitated by policy experts who set up conditions for collaboration and iterative policy development.

In each of these two different approaches, the role of the policymakers is distinct. In the first scenario, policymakers gather information and present evidence-informed arguments for policy options. In the second scenario, policymakers guide stakeholder groups to develop policy through deliberation and design processes. Each approach is legitimate and has its place. Yet, rational policymaking, as demonstrated in the first scenario, dominates education decision-making. Current policymakers know little about how to use deliberation and engagement to make policy. This chapter focuses on how we can develop more deliberative policymakers, such as those described in the second scenario, to supplement (and, when needed, offset) the predominance of the rational policymakers.

For an analogy on which to design new policymaking roles, it is useful to look to the world of foreign affairs and the art of statecraft. Statecraft is the ability to manage complicated political negotiations and agreements between nation-states, which suggests intense personal engagement with people and problems. Statesmen and stateswomen often jet back and forth between world capitals to negotiate directly with leaders in a process of public and private diplomacy. Statecraft suggests a seriousness and importance in the manner of the work, evoking characteristics of wise judgment, practical knowledge, political savvy, and leadership. Statecraft is of a different character than analysis and is about governance and the process of organizing institutions and practices to solve problems, communicate, and build understanding.[2] In an education policy context, statecraft would similarly use diplomacy, deep engagement, and skillful management of public affairs to support a process of deliberative policymaking.

In his argument for policymaking in a democracy, social scientist Robert Reich describes a policymaking role that is about stimulating public deliberation over what is good for society rather than deciding specific policy.[3] Reich contends that deliberation and public learning are at least as important as policymaking. John Dewey argued along the same lines, stating that the essential need of democracy "is the improvement of the methods and conditions of debate, discussion and persuasion."[4] Statecraft is the ability to bring people together to solve problems. Employing statecraft in education policymaking would give us more than one model to draw from when creating policy.

The rational decision model, with its emphasis on efficiency and effectiveness, has been with us for decades. In 1970, the economist and scholar Alice Rivlin, who later led the newly created Congressional Budget Office and then the Office of Management and Budget, wrote a short treatise titled *Systematic Thinking for Social Action* that argued for a rational decision-making approach in government.[5] Rivlin was among a wave of policy experts who entered government after the surfeit of social legislation in the mid-1960s and, with a number of other critical observers, noted the flaws in those federal policies. She wrote of those early programs that they were based on "hunches and theories," as there were few facts and little was known about how to effectively address poverty. Title I of the Elementary and Secondary Education Act was a $1 billion a year program that, she states, "was passed largely on faith."[6] With very little knowledge of how to run compensatory programs, Rivlin notes that "the educator hoped for significant improvement in the average performance of poor children. The analyst hoped that something would be learned from the experience. Both have been largely disappointed." The response to these disappointments among many early scholars was to press for using the scientific method. The systematic thinking approach pressed policymakers to develop evidence, use well-designed experiments, conduct random control trials and evaluation studies, and analyze costs and benefits. The rational decision model that policymakers championed then and is the basis of our policymaking even now is one of ordering alternative policies, gathering information on the advantages and disadvantages of each, and estimating the costs and benefits of public action mixed with judgment and attention to important values.

The second model, the deliberative model of policymaking, would include the skills and dispositions of the democrat in partnership with those of the technocrat. Beyond drafting and deciding rules and regulations, policymakers would take on a facilitative role of engaging the public in the process. A facilitator leads a group forward by helping its members work better together and create common understandings of their goals and the policymaking process. In this model, the role of policymakers and policy analysts is to not only make decisions that are responsive to public desires, as Reich argues, but also take on the greater challenge of engaging the public "in ongoing dialogue over what problems should be addressed, what is at stake in such decisions, and how to strengthen the public's capacities" to deal with public problems.[7] A new education statecraft expands the expectations of policymakers skilled in policy analysis to an expectation that they are also skilled in policy facilitation. Like the actions in foreign policy, education statecraft means intense personal engagement to build understanding, gather evidence of what is happening on the ground, and implement strategies.

Rather than setting out an overarching theory to guide policy content, statecraft focuses on actions necessary to address each problem as it arises. There are no overriding principles to guide reform. This approach stands in stark contrast to current practice in education policymaking, which has for decades focused on developing the next policy grand strategy. No Child Left Behind had a grand strategy. In simplified form, the strategy was to measure school performance and pressure low-performing schools to improve; consequently, children's achievement would improve. Race to the Top had a grand strategy to develop rigorous standards and assessments, adopt better data systems, turn around low-performing schools, and support great teachers and leaders. The Every Student Succeeds Act has a less grand strategy but nonetheless puts forward a version of previous accountability theories and pushes decision-making to states and localities. The challenge with grand strategies, however, is that they simplify the complexities of education improvement. While big ideas and intellectual frameworks may provide essential organizing structures, they are challenged by the day-to-day demand for more down-to-earth policy skills.[8] Rather than setting out an overarching theory to guide policy content, statecraft focuses on actions necessary to address each problem as it arises.

Current training prepares analysts to take their place in currently structured policymaking rather than lead in building processes that reach a higher standard of delivering deliberation, civic capacity, and social learning. We must both rationally decide and deliberatively design our way to better policy. Much of our policy training today is missing the mechanics of an education statecraft. If we are to have different policymaking, we need different policymakers, those who are masters of both sets of critical skills: the technocrat and the democrat.

After seeing decades of rational policymaking unfold, Rivlin, in hindsight, hinted at a different philosophy of policymaking. Looking again at policymaking practices forty-five years after her original writing, she notes that in working through interventions to improve social conditions through the late 1960s and early 1970s, "it gradually dawned on all of us that progress was going to be complicated and would require continuous learning and adjustment."[9] "The process of developing new methods, trying them out, modifying them, trying again, will have to be continuous," she concluded.[10] Her message to a passionate audience eager for social action was to slow down and take time to learn from experience. We are still learning how best to do that in our policymaking processes.

A NEW BREED OF POLICYMAKER

Because policymaking actions themselves have an impact, separate even from the effect of policy, the role of people in public policymaking positions is grander than we had imagined. Their actions in policymaking and the processes they build are consequential. Thus, our training for these roles must be greater than at present. Rather than entering the field as a policy analyst, skilled at pulling apart the weaknesses of an existing policy and weighing policy alternatives for the future, a new breed of policymakers would enter the field as facilitators skilled in managing deliberatively democratic practices that develop shared learning and build civic capacity in the process of policy development.

Training policymakers in statecraft would shift the balance of expected know-how from that of policymaker as expert to policymaker as designer and facilitator. With that shift comes an emphasis on a new set of skills oriented toward understanding education policy design, facilitating public deliberation, building useful feedback systems, partnering effectively with policy intermediaries, creating effective conditions for implementation, and facilitating the development of shared knowledge.

Today's graduate education policy programs are not structured or equipped to produce a new and more deliberative breed of policymaker. The vast majority of graduate education programs are oriented toward economic and political science philosophies of policy analysis. Coursework consists of classes in the economics of education policy, the politics of education policy, policy analysis, and quantitative methods. These courses are the policy sciences canon. The graduate school at RAND, established in 1970, was one of the original public policy schools. RAND's graduate work was grounded in economic theory and focused on solving problems through the federal government. RAND had been one of the first schools to teach the "systematic thinking" described by Alice Rivlin as it sought to extend rational policy analysis beyond its original use in the military to address civil issues such as education and health.[11] Recently, however, there has been a shift toward teaching a new style of policymaking at RAND and other sites around the country.

In 2020, a group of public policy educators, including leading academics, deans, and former public officials, drafted the "Statement on Education for Public Problem Solving" that sounded an alarm about an eroding public capability to solve problems through democratic governance.[12] The authors argue that "the system of educating and training people to solve public problems is radically insufficient" and they call for new approaches. These approaches include drawing heavily on local history and context to identify problems, using methods of policy design, and attending to implementation that learns from others and expects constant adaptation amid experiments.[13] Their statement affirms the need for new policymakers with a different sense of identity and mindset toward their work.

Interestingly, the Pardee RAND Graduate School is today leading the way in redesigning training for policymakers. In 2020, RAND accepted its first doctoral cohort into a "reinvented" policy PhD program.[14] The new program includes a community-partnered policy and action stream of study focused on working with community partners to design, implement, and evaluate policies. While the program includes traditional coursework in economic and quantitative analysis, it emphasizes applied learning in a project-based policy design studio and in long-running community partnerships.

Stanford University's International Policy program has also added coursework in human-centered design and built in a practical problem-solving component focused on following the policy process through to implementation and change. The master's capstone practicum has students work with community partners to solve current problems. The director of the program, political scientist Francis Fukuyama, describes the skills students need as those that go beyond analyzing problems and manipulating data to being able to formulate and implement solutions under real-world conditions.[15]

These and other innovative programs have acknowledged that one of the consequences of enshrining scientific policy analysis in graduate education programs is that it empowers scientifically oriented experts at the expense of both bureaucratic managers and citizens. As policy scholars Anne L. Schneider and Helen Ingram argue in their book on *Policy Design for Democracy*, policy communities made up of educated specialists "dominate the setting of the agenda, terms of debate, and alternatives being considered," and by operating through small networks to make policy, the "laypersons who lack specialized knowledge and command of the appropriate jargon are treated as outsiders."[16] The sophistication and complexity of policy analyses tends to discourage wide participation, as few people feel they have much to add to a debate of this kind.[17] One of the consequences of centering scientific policy analysis is that it limits the participation and contributions of practitioners who are actually engaged in the work. Schneider and Ingram warn that under these conditions, citizens become spectators, and "government comes to be a conversation among the few that is irrelevant to the many."[18]

The logic behind policy design thinking challenges both the culture of current policy decision-making and the structures, particularly within government agencies, that are built to further rational policymaking processes. For example, in order to partner with education policy intermediaries in the development process, policymakers will have to surrender key elements of authority over decision-making.[19] As thinkers in this tradition have noted, these practices will require significant cultural change and capacity building within government, especially as the goal is to reshape policymaking as more democratic and participatory rather than simply generate innovative ideas.[20]

A SIGNATURE PEDAGOGY

Across the previous chapters, I've argued that new policymaking activities—using principles of human-centered design, harnessing the role of intermediaries, placing implementation at the forefront, and engaging in a new style of federal-state relations—will create the conditions for democratic participation and social learning in policymaking and produce better policy decisions. With this aim, the graduate school challenge becomes, in the words of Lee Shulman, president emeritus of the Carnegie Foundation, that of determining the "signature pedagogy" for the practice of policy, that is, what counts as a policymakers' knowledge and how those things become known.[21] A signature pedagogy includes the content of coursework and the style of instruction as well as the implicit understandings of what constitutes expertise and where authority rests. If lawyers learn to think like lawyers through the Socratic method, the question for policy training is that of how policy leaders might learn to govern and make policy within a new model of statecraft.

New policymaking will require among new policymakers a different identity and mindset toward the work. The switch in identity will compel a focus on "coordination, knowledge accreditation and stewardship rather than delivery and control" in order to effectively address public problems.[22] Therefore, a signature pedagogy for a new education statecraft must grapple with challenges to traditional power and expertise. There are sociopolitical implications in a user-centered, participatory style of policymaking that have to be part of the conversation. A new notion of expertise must exist and be respected across policy actors and layperson participants. In the Kentucky example at the top of the chapter, the policy facilitators deliberately defined expertise broadly and worked to increase knowledge across the board so that the power differences between traditional experts and citizens were reduced.[23] The traditional role of expert is thus somewhat upended.

As the "Statement on Education for Public Problem Solving" acknowledges, we do not have a signature pedagogy. The authors note that "we do not yet have a common program for how to teach all this—how to find the right balance of historical understanding, social science tools and insights, moral reasoning, design methods, fieldwork, and various practical skills." Yet, within the notion of the new education statecraft as presented in earlier chapters, there are suggestions of which direction to take. Among them are an emphasis on the capabilities of facilitating design processes, engaging deeply with stakeholders, working with policy intermediary organizations, leading public deliberation, and implementation planning.

Policy Design Thinking

As important as the content within policy design training are the experiences of actually doing the work. One of the policymakers' tasks is to facilitate policy design thinking processes and deliberatively democratic engagements on policy issues.[24] Some of the most important aspects of democratic governance involve creating opportunities for the public to deliberate about what is good for society. Yet, as the economist Elinor Ostrom notes, few students of policy analysis see their study as informing themselves on how to become better citizens. She cautioned that "by removing decisions about the ways to innovate, adapt, and coordinate efforts from those who are directly affected . . . policy reforms have created institutions that are less able to respond to the problems for which they were created."[25] A new education statecraft expands the policymaker's job from that of making or implementing policy choices to participating in democratic governing processes that continuously articulate public values and stimulate public deliberation.[26]

The new graduate program at RAND is building long-term partnerships with community agencies as settings for public problem solving and graduate training. The coursework includes a practicum focused on policy development and implementation and a community partnership dissertation requirement. There is a course on engaging communities in research that links research skill development with community-based research. Another course on dissemination and research focuses on community information and participation needs and the practice of translating evidence in partnership with communities. Yet another course focuses on working on short-term projects with clients. Policy labs also provide opportunities to put design into practice. As described in chapter 3, dozens of policy design labs exist around the world. Like education lab schools that were often established by universities to test new forms of instruction, policy labs test new forms of public idea development and decision-making.

Widening inclusion of participation in policymaking, regardless of the extent of that participation, requires that traditional policymakers be immersed in particular policy contexts.[27] The facilitation and engagement means that there is a level of embeddedness among participants and thus the need to have skills for leading and managing processes closer to the microlevel of deliberation than the macrolevel of policy development. This suggests training in deliberative democracy theory but also in practical application with communities through understanding of negotiation, collaboration, and facilitation. It would also recommend training in partnership management or coalition building as would happen with policy intermediaries.

CONCLUSION

When faced with situations of great cognitive complexity, such as those that face contemporary education policymakers, the rational response is learning.[28] As the policy philosopher Giandemenico Majone suggests, the rationality of public policymaking depends more on improving the learning capacity of the various organs of public deliberation than on maximizing achievement of particular goals."[29] If we are to deliberate and design our way to better education policy, we need different education policymakers. Rather than policy analysts, we need policy facilitators.

Given that a new education statecraft is still uncertain territory, there isn't a canon of tried-and-true learning that can be immediately taken up in new policy training. Our next steps will need to include the process of inquiry into these methods themselves in order to build that body of knowledge. Fortunately, in some governments and some graduate schools that work is moving forward. As this work progresses, educators will need to consider how coursework and practical experience create a signature pedagogy that facilitates more than just the development of effective policies, even as this is at the core of policy practice. The pedagogy must include theoretical and applied foundations of democracy, citizenship, and governance in combination with research, analysis, and design.

CHAPTER EIGHT

Deliberation and Policymaking

AFTER YEARS OF EXPERIENCE with education policy—implementing policy as a school principal, analyzing policy as a researcher, informing policy as an education advocate, and writing policy as a federal policymaker—I can perhaps in one sentence sum up what I've learned: Even with the smartest people at the table, the manner in which we choose to make policy matters.

At the start of the book, I described the smallness of policymaking tables at the federal level and how decisions made by the smart, talented people seated at those tables are often unable to meet the demands of our time. This same scenario plays out at the state and local level, and while the size and scope of the policy decisions being made are different, all are operating under the same assumption: a formal policy decision that is based on reliable data and analysis will set in motion the desired changes. Unfortunately, no matter how well engineered those changes are, the policy goals we hope to further are often hamstrung by an underlying architecture of beliefs and practices. That is the technical challenge we face. There is a moral challenge as well. It is irresponsible for a small group of people to make policy that is so detached from educators and communities. To fully acknowledge and alter these beliefs and practices, education policymaking needs to dig deeper.

There are ways we can reshape and reinvigorate policymaking activities so they strengthen our collective capacity to arrive at and implement better education policies. Though the focus of this book is on federal and state policymaking, the lessons may be applicable across policymaking situations and experiences. The fundamental methods considered in this book and summarized in this chapter rely on the principles of human-centered design, place implementation at the forefront, and engage in a new style of federal-state relations. These ideas push federal and state policymakers toward more broadly democratic actions, from the ground up, to shape policy decisions. In essence, they encourage more and larger tables for policymaking.

DELIBERATIVE POLICYMAKING

Civic capacity posits that educational reform will not be successful without shared community knowledge that supports the collective action of multiple participants. The concept of community cognition in civic decisions and civic mobilization is important for rethinking policymaking. Community cognition emphasizes the shared learning and accumulated knowledge required to mobilize broad support for education reforms. Scholars of civic capacity suggest that reform is built on communal and sustained civic effort that has the political wherewithal to upend traditional relationships and structures and to create new patterns and behaviors that will better serve schools. Without civic capacity to initiate and sustain improvement efforts, progress on systemic improvements is sluggish or ineffective.[1] The policymaking system that we have now does not set the political and community conditions needed for education improvement even if the policy content is on target.

Understandably, the traditional focus of policymakers is content, the analysis of what has worked and what hasn't, and the political dynamics of decision-making. We must now add to this body of work a better understanding of how we can more effectively develop that content and, in that development process, build the conditions necessary for policy success. This kind of deliberative policymaking can generate civic capacity and build a shared understanding of what is required for education reform. Along with creating civic capacity, deliberative policymaking helps cultivate the conditions for successful implementation.

Policy Design Thinking

Through the design thinking process, the human experience becomes central to judging the value of solutions. From empathy building to iterative prototype testing, the stages of user-centered design force the designer to attend to people's needs, experiences, and preferences. As a frame for education policymaking, the design process helps policy actors recognize the complicated realities intrinsic to educational settings and place human needs and capabilities first.

Policy shifts from being an end product to a prototype, or hypothesis, that is meant to be tested and improved. At the end of the design cycle, prototype testing establishes the feedback loop needed to refine a policy hypothesis closer to a policy solution. The cumulative cycles of build, test, see, and refine are a way to accelerate learning and quicken feedback loops.[2] Through design thinking, implementation becomes an equally weighted step within the whole of an iterative improvement process.

Policy design thinking provides a formal human-centered problem-solving process that can bolster civic approaches to policymaking. This approach attends to the context and conditions of education challenges and builds feedback into the process. The tools of design thinking increase opportunities for broad community learning as policy activities move from elite offices to more democratic and inclusive settings. The approach holds the promise of expanding social learning broadly across a community and with stakeholders in particular. Among those stakeholders are the educators and leaders who implement policy decisions.

Implementation at the Forefront

Placing implementation at the forefront—attending to the form and practice of implementation in the early steps of policy design—brings implementation into the larger understanding of policymaking affirmed through the arguments in this book: that policymaking ought to deepen democracy, civic capacity, and social learning even while it achieves improved outcomes. Social learning is critical for policy development and education reform efforts. It is key to implementation.[3] Implementation hinges on social understanding and the process of making sense of policy in order to change practice.[4] Policymaking can either skip the learning processes, as in our current practices, or embed them within the policy process.

Placing implementation at the forefront of policymaking requires us to acknowledge implementation as an ongoing act, one that requires interactions where the parties negotiate and renegotiate, or coconstruct, the meaning of the policy and implementation over time. Through this process of politics and compromise, participants construct a new version of policy at the ground level. This kind of continual improvement process forgoes the separation between creation and implementation. Instead, we engage in a whole and continuous process rather than separate steps done by separate groups of people. Policy decisions must not miss users' needs and the challenges of implementation.

Harnessing the Role of Intermediaries

A new approach to policymaking, organized around design thinking and implementation at the forefront, requires new structures that articulate democratic and design-oriented policy spaces. These activities require a new public square or, more accurately, multiple new public squares where the actions of deliberative policymaking and social learning take place. Education policy intermediaries are positioned to create those more productive policy spaces.

The ask of education policy intermediaries is that they take on the extra weight of supporting a deliberative process, that as policy actors they do not simply suggest solutions or inform policymakers but instead create distinctive practices of public deliberation that help us determine where the public interest lies and what our common obligations are. Among the many implications of broadened participation in education policy is a concern that knowledgeable policymakers involve an inclusive constituency to project and protect the collective intent.[5]

Relational Federalism

By design, the structure of the US public education system challenges the ideals of design thinking, deliberation, and civic capacity. While many aspects of education (standards, curriculum, local governance) are determined by states, the federal government has an important and consequential role to play. But the ever-present tension between state decision-making and federal law (as exemplified with the No Child Left Behind and Race to the Top programs) makes mutual learning and iterative policymaking all but impossible. It is important to remember, however, that most federal policies are built on state experience. By centering policy arguments around the allocation of power at the federal level or autonomy at the state level, we miss the chance to harness the inherent interdependence among federal, state, and local actors. A relational view of federal-state power dynamics raises the possibility of policy reaping the benefits of mutual learning, iteration, and healthy competition that are part of a shoulder-to-shoulder relational struggle.[6]

Education Statecraft

If we are to improve education policy, we must teach policymaking in a broader and more expansive manner. For decades, a rational economics-driven approach to policy analysis and design has dominated graduate education programs. Curriculum focuses on statistical analysis, cost-benefit analysis, and the pursuit of efficient policy options. Yet, real policymaking has little in common with this kind of approach. Public engagement, context, communication, and advocacy all contribute to shaping existing rules and regulations. To advance effective policy today, policymakers must struggle with and become skilled at meeting the moral, ethical, and democratic demands of public stewardship.

Current policy training isn't wrong; it is just incomplete. We envision and teach an underconceptualized understanding of policymaking. In my own experience and in conversations with colleagues and policy professionals, we note that policymakers should first and foremost enter their positions with the skills needed to facilitate policy development: moving ideas to implementation, engaging in community and intermediary partnerships, and increasing social learning, that shared community knowledge that supports collective action and is critical to policy development, reform, implementation and sustainability. Policy training must include the skills and dispositions of the democrat in concert with those of the technocrat.

FINAL THOUGHTS AND A CALL TO ACTION

Policymaking presents us with challenges and opportunities in equal measure. At its best, policymaking is an instrument of democracy. It can build awareness and understanding and strengthen the collective capacity of individuals and communities. But all too often, policymaking lacks the kind of shared learning and purposeful action needed to support improvements and transformational change.

Democracy and equity demand attention in our policymaking. Structural inequities, particularly racial inequities, and unequal participation indicate that it is a critical time to revive democracy and democratic participation. The imbalance of political control between citizens and decision-makers, represented in populist arguments, is as apparent in education policy discussions as in broader national political currents. Although the demands of our time complicate the already challenging job of policymakers, current practices overlook the opportunities that policymaking can foster. Policymaking can serve democracy through deliberative processes that are inclusive and build a collective capacity to solve public problems. Policymaking can deepen social learning and cultivate conditions for successful implementation.

In previous chapters I made the distinction between decision-makers who make final choices and enshrine policy choices into law or regulation and policymakers who supply policy ideas, language, or reasoning to decision-makers; the distinction is important for expanding policymaking beyond limited decision tables. Likewise, in a push for more deliberative policymaking, the demand side is critical. Legislative and executive decision-makers have the ability to question how policies are developed and expect more thorough user-centered, ground-up, implementation-ready policies. In fact, it is the demand from decision-makers for a more complete policy process that will stimulate change. If decision-makers are unwilling to accept policy ideas that arrive without a provenance in deliberative process, then those who supply policy ideas, including advocates and policy entrepreneurs in intermediary organizations, will be more inclined to undertake the effort. By demanding a better process before receiving the supply of policy input, decision-makers encourage deliberation and the growth of civic capacity in the actions themselves.

If we ever hope to fully realize an equitable and high-performing public education system that serves all students, we need to reshape the policymaking landscape. The policy cycle has many steps—agenda setting, formulation, enactment, implementation, evaluation—and each fosters its own voluminous research and theory. Yet, in seeing the process as a whole rather than as disconnected pieces, policymakers can purposefully use the policymaking process itself as an important lever of change.

Notes

CHAPTER 1

1. David T. Conley, *The Common Core State Standards: Insight into Their Development and Purpose* (Washington, DC: Council of Chief State School Officers, 2014); and Jason Zimba, "The Development and Design of the Common Core State Standards for Mathematics," *New England Journal of Public Policy* 26, no. 1, article 10 (September 2014): 1–11.
2. Michele McNeil and Sean Cavanagh, "Expert Panels Named in Common-Standards Push," *Education Week*, July 1, 2009, https://www.edweek.org/policy-politics/expert-panels-named-in-common-standards-push/2009/07.
3. Catherine Gewertz, "The Common Core Explained," *Education Week*, September 30, 2015, https://www.edweek.org/teaching-learning/the-common-core-explained/2015/09; Rick Hess, "Did I Accurately Guess the Fate of the Common Core? You Be the Judge," *Education Week*, August 1, 2022, https://www.edweek.org/teaching-learning/opinion-did-i-accurately-guess-the-fate-of-the-common-core-you-be-the-judge/2022/08; and Sara Schwartz, "The Architects of the Standards Movement Say They Missed a Big Piece," *Education Week*, November 28, 2022, https://www.edweek.org/teaching-learning/the-architects-of-the-standards-movement-say-they-missed-a-big-piece/2022/11.
4. Hess, "Did I Accurately Guess the Fate of the Common Core?"
5. David A. Gamson, Kathryn A. McDermott, and Douglas S. Reed, "The Elementary and Secondary Education Act at Fifty: Aspirations, Effects, and Limitations," *RSF: The Russell Sage Foundation Journal of the Social Sciences* 1, no. 3 (2015): 1–29.
6. Dorothy Shipps, "The Politics of Educational Reform: Idea Champions and Policy Windows," in *Shaping Education Policy*, ed. Douglas E. Mitchell, Robert L. Crowson, and Dorothy Shipps, 259–85 (New York: Routledge, 2011).
7. Milbrey Wallin McLaughlin, *Evaluation and Reform: The Elementary and Secondary Education Act of 1965, Title I* (Santa Monica, CA: Rand, 1974); and Paul Berman and Milbrey Wallin McLaughlin, *Federal Programs Supporting Education Change: A Model of Educational Change* (Santa Monica, CA: Rand, 1974).

8. James J. Heckman et al., "The Rate of Return to the HighScope Perry Preschool Program," *Journal of Public Economics* 94, no. 1–2 (2010): 114–28; James J. Heckman and Ganesh Karapakula, *Intergenerational and Intragenerational Externalities of the Perry Preschool Project* (Cambridge, MA: National Bureau of Economic Research, 2019), https://www.nber.org/papers/w25888.
9. Gamson, McDermott, and Reed, "The Elementary and Secondary Education Act at Fifty."
10. Shipps, "The Politics of Educational Reform," 280.
11. David Leonhardt, Amanda Cox, and Claire Cain Miller, "An Atlas of Upward Mobility Shows Paths Out of Poverty," *New York Times*, May 4, 2015, https://www.nytimes.com/2015/05/04/upshot/an-atlas-of-upward-mobility-shows-paths-out-of-poverty.html.
12. Sara Mervosh, "The Pandemic Erased Two Decades of Progress in Math and Reading," *New York Times*, September 1, 2022, https://www.nytimes.com/2022/09/01/us/national-test-scores-math-reading-pandemic.html.
13. "Reading and Mathematics Scores Decline during COVID-19 Pandemic," The Nation's Report Card, 2022, https://www.nationsreportcard.gov/highlights/ltt/2022/.
14. Louis Menand, *The Metaphysical Club: A Story of Ideas in America* (New York: Macmillan, 2002), 440–41.
15. David K. Cohen and Jal D. Mehta, "Why Reform Sometimes Succeeds: Understanding the Conditions That Produce Reforms That Last," *American Educational Research Journal* 54, no. 4 (2017): 644–90; and Azad Singh Bali, Giliberto Capano, and M. Ramesh, "Anticipating and Designing for Policy Effectiveness," *Policy and Society* 38, no. 1 (2019): 1–13.
16. Clarence N. Stone, Jeffrey R. Henig, Bryan D. Jones, and Carol Pierannunzi, *Building Civic Capacity: The Politics of Reforming Urban Schools* (Lawrence: University Press of Kansas, 2001), 122.
17. Stone et al., *Building Civic Capacity*, 1–9.
18. Stone et al., *Building Civic Capacity*, 126.
19. Clarence N. Stone, "Efficiency versus Social Learning: A Reconsideration of the Implementation Process," *Review of Policy Research* 4, no. 3 (1985): 486.
20. Jonathan Rauch, *The Constitution of Knowledge: A Defense of Truth* (Washington, DC: Brookings Institution Press, 2021), 3 (emphasis added).
21. Cynthia E. Coburn, "Rethinking Scale: Moving beyond Numbers to Deep and Lasting Change," *Educational Researcher* 32, no. 6 (2003): 3–12.
22. Craig W. Shinn, "Civic Capacity: Theory, Research and Practice," *Administrative Theory & Praxis* 21, no. 1 (1999): 103–19.
23. Amy Gutmann and Dennis F. Thompson, *Why Deliberative Democracy?* (Princeton, NJ: Princeton University Press, 2009), 1–63.
24. Gutmann and Thompson, *Why Deliberative Democracy?*, 9.

25. Yannis Papadopoulos, "On the Embeddedness of Deliberative Systems: Why Elitist Innovations Matter More," in *Deliberative Systems: Deliberative Democracy at the Large Scale*, ed. John Parkinson and Jane Mansbridge, 125–50 (Cambridge: Cambridge University Press, 2012).
26. Elizabeth Anderson, "The Epistemology of Democracy," *Episteme: A Journal of Social Epistemology* 3, no. 1 (2006): 8–22; and Hélène Landemore, "Collective Wisdom: Old and New," in *Collective Wisdom: Principles and Mechanisms*, ed. Hélène Landemore and Jon Elster, 1–20 (Cambridge: Cambridge University Press, 2012); Hélène Landemore, *Democratic Reason: Politics, Collective Intelligence, and the Rule of the Many* (Princeton, NJ: Princeton University Press, 2012), 1–26.
27. Anderson, "The Epistemology of Democracy."
28. Anderson, "The Epistemology of Democracy."
29. Robert B. Reich, *The Power of Public Ideas* (Cambridge: Harvard University Press, 1990), 1–29.
30. Joshua Cohen and Archon Fung, "Radical Democracy," *Swiss Journal of Political Science* 10, no. 4 (Winter 2004): 23–34.
31. John S. Dryzek et al., "The Crisis of Democracy and the Science of Deliberation," *Science* 363, no. 6432 (2019): 1144–46.
32. See Papadopoulos, "On the Embeddedness of Deliberative Systems."
33. Reich, *The Power of Public Ideas*; Francis Fukuyama, "What's Wrong with Public Policy Education," The American Interest, August 1, 2018, https://www.the-american-interest.com/2018/08/01/whats-wrong-with-public-policy-education/; and Malcolm Burley, "How the Harvard Kennedy School Abandoned America," *Boston Magazine*, January 22, 2017, https://www.bostonmagazine.com/news/2017/01/22/harvard-kennedy-school-america/.

CHAPTER 2

1. Edwin O. Guthman and C. Richard Allen, *RFK: His Words for Our Times* (New York: William Morrow, 2018), 266.
2. Guthman and Allen, *RFK*, 272.
3. Evan Thomas, *Robert Kennedy: His Life* (New York: Simon and Schuster, 2002), 323.
4. Giandomenico Majone, "Policies as Theories," *Omega* 8, no. 2 (1980): 153–54.
5. Guthman and Allen, *RFK*, 273.
6. Guthman and Allen, 231.
7. Hugh Davis Graham, *The Transformation of Federal Education Policy: The Kennedy and Johnson Years* (Washington, DC: National Institute of Education, 1983), 375.
8. Graham, *The Transformation of Federal Education Policy*, 162.

9. Milbrey Wallin McLaughlin, *Evaluation and Reform: The Elementary and Secondary Education Act of 1965, Title I* (Santa Monica, CA: Rand Corporation, 1974), 3.
10. McLaughlin, *Evaluation and Reform*, 3.
11. McLaughlin, *Evaluation and Reform*, v.
12. Majone, "Policies as Theories," 152–55.
13. Michael D. Shear and Daniel de Vise, "Obama Announces $12 Billion Community College Initiative," *Washington Post*, July 15, 2009, https://www.washingtonpost.com/wp-dyn/content/article/2009/07/14/AR2009071400819_2.html?sid=ST2009071502758.
14. James G. Cibulka, "Policy Analysis and the Study of the Politics of Education," *Journal of Education Policy* 9, no. 5 (1994): 106.
15. Louis Menand, *The Metaphysical Club: A Story of Ideas in America* (New York: Farrar, Straus, and Giroux, 2002), 146.
16. Archon Fung, "Varieties of Participation in Complex Governance," *Public Administration Review* 66 (2006), 73.
17. Frances Fox Piven and Richard Cloward, *Poor People's Movements: Why They Succeed, How They Fail* (New York: Vintage Books, 2012), 23.
18. John Arnold Kingdon, *Agendas, Alternatives, and Public Policies*, updated 2nd ed. (Glenview, IL: Pearson Education, 2011).
19. Kingdon, *Agendas, Alternatives, and Public Policies,* 110.
20. Clarence N. Stone et al., *Building Civic Capacity: The Politics of Reforming Urban Schools* (Lawrence: University Press of Kansas, 2001), 102.
21. Kingdon, *Agendas, Alternatives, and Public Policies*, 86–89.
22. Bob Hudson, David Hunter, and Stephen Peckham, "Policy Failure and the Policy-Implementation Gap: Can Policy Support Programs Help?," *Policy Design and Practice* 2, no. 1 (2019): 3–4.
23. Milbrey Wallin McLaughlin, "Learning from Experience: Lessons from Policy Implementation," *Educational Evaluation and Policy Analysis* 9, no. 2 (1987): 171–78; and Marshall S. Smith and Jennifer O'Day, "Systemic School Reform," in *The Politics of Curriculum and Testing*, ed. Susan H Fuhrman and Betty Malen, 233–67 (New York: Falmer, 1991).
24. David K. Cohen and James P. Spillane, "Policy and Practice: The Relations Between Governance and Instruction," *Review of Research in Education* 18 (1992): 40.
25. James P. Spillane, Brian J. Reiser, and Louis M. Gomez, "Policy Implementation and Cognition," in *New Directions in Educational Policy Implementation*, ed. Meredith I. Honig, 47–64 (New York: SUNY Press, 2006).
26. Amanda Datnow, "Connections in the Policy Chain: The 'Co-Construction' of Implementation in Comprehensive School Reform," in *New Directions in Education Policy Implementation*, ed. Meredith I. Honig, 105–23 (New York:

SUNY Press, 2006); and Jenny Stewart, *The Dilemmas of Engagement: The Role of Consultation in Governance* (Canberra, Australia: ANU Press, 2009).

27. Kara Swisher, "Why 3rd Grade Matters," November 19, 2020, https://www.nytimes.com/2020/11/19/opinion/sway-kara-swisher-raj-chetty.html?action=click&module=audio-series-bar®ion=header&pgtype=Article; and Peter Bergman et al., "Creating Moves to Opportunity: Experimental Evidence on Barriers to Neighborhood Choice," MAL National Bureau of Economic Research working paper no. 26164, August 2019, https://www.nber.org/system/files/working_papers/w26164/w26164.pdf.
28. Christopher T. Cross, *Political Education: National Policy Comes of Age*, updated ed. (New York: Teachers College Press, 2010), 29.
29. McLaughlin, *Evaluation and Reform*, 59–65.
30. John Dewey, *The Public and Its Problems: An Essay in Political Inquiry* (Athens: Ohio University Press, 2016), 220.
31. Jill S. Cannon et al., "Investing Early: Taking Stock of Outcomes and Economic Returns from Early Childhood Programs," *Rand Health Quarterly* 7, no. 4 (2018); and James J. Heckman et al., "The Rate of Return to the HighScope Perry Preschool Program," *Journal of Public Economics* 94, nos. 1–2 (2010): 114–28.
32. Lynn A. Karoly et al., "Decades of Evidence Demonstrate That Early Childhood Programs Can Benefit Children and Provide Economic Returns," Research brief, Rand Corporation, 2017, https://www.rand.org/content/dam/rand/pubs/research_briefs/RB9900/RB9993/RAND_RB9993.pdf.
33. Atul Gawande, *Better: A Surgeon's Notes on Performance* (New York: Metropolitan Books, 2007), 8.
34. Stone et al., *Building Civic Capacity*, 27.
35. David B. Tyack, *The One Best System: A History of American Urban Education* (Cambridge, MA: Harvard University Press, 1974).
36. Stone et al., *Building Civic Capacity*, 1.
37. Stone et al., 2.
38. Robert B. Reich, ed., *The Power of Public Ideas* (Cambridge, MA: Harvard University Press, 1990), 4.
39. Anthony S. Bryk et al., *How a City Learned to Improve Its Schools* (Cambridge, MA: Harvard Education Press, 2023), 278–84.
40. Stone et al., *Building Civic Capacity*, 17–19.
41. Stone et al., *Building Civic Capacity*, 1–9.
42. Tyack, *The One Best System*, 272.
43. William Genieys, "C. Wright Mills, *The Power Elite*," in *The Oxford Handbook of Classics in Public Policy and Administration*, ed. Steven J. Balla, Martin Lodge, and Edward C. Page, 69–79 (Oxford: Oxford University Press, 2016).
44. Jeremy Heimans and Henry Timms, "Understanding 'New Power,'" *Harvard Business Review* 92, no. 12 (2014): 48–56.

45. Dewey, *The Public and Its Problems*, 223.
46. Heimans and Timms, "Understanding 'New Power,'" 51–52.
47. Heimans and Timms, "Understanding 'New Power,'" 51.
48. Heimans and Timms, "Understanding 'New Power'"; and Michael Lind, "Saving Democracy from the Managerial Elite," *The Wall Street Journal*, January 10, 2020, https://www.wsj.com/articles/saving-democracy-from-the-managerial-elite-11578672945?mod=hp_lista_pos1.
49. Carolyn G. Heilbrun, *Writing a Woman's Life* (New York: Norton, 2008), 18.
50. Archon Fung, "Four Levels of Power: A Conception to Enable Liberation," *Journal of Political Philosophy* 28, no. 2 (2020): 131–57.
51. Lind, "Saving Democracy from the Managerial Elite."

CHAPTER 3

1. "Aeron: The Best Selling Office Chair," *Smart Furniture Blog*, March 23, 2021, https://blog.smartfurniture.com/products-aeron-chair-best-selling-chair/.
2. Cliff Kuang, "The Secret History of the Aeron Chair," Slate, November 5, 2012, https://slate.com/human-interest/2012/11/aeron-chair-history-herman-millers-office-staple-was-originally-designed-for-the-elderly.html.
3. Kuang, "The Secret History of the Aeron Chair."
4. The bracketed term is in the original.
5. "Design Q & A: Bill Stumpf," *WHY Magazine*, updated August 1, 2021, https://www.hermanmiller.com/stories/why-magazine/design-q-and-a-bill-stumpf/.
6. Kuang, "The Secret History of the Aeron Chair."
7. Don Norman, *The Design of Everyday Things*, revised and expanded ed. (New York: Basic Books, 2013), 8.
8. John S. Gero, "Design Prototypes: A Knowledge Representation Schema for Design," *AI Magazine* 11, no. 4 (1990): 26–36.
9. Tom Bentley, "Design in Policy: Challenges and Sources of Hope for Policymakers," in *Design for Policy*, ed. Christian Bason (New York: Routledge, 2014), 15.
10. Bentley, "Design in Policy."
11. Chad Aldeman, "The Teacher Evaluation Revamp, in Hindsight: What the Obama Administration's Signature Reform Got Wrong," *Education Next* 17, no. 2 (2017): 60–68.
12. Aldeman, "The Teacher Evaluation Revamp," 66–68.
13. Aldeman, "The Teacher Evaluation Revamp," 62.
14. Maria Ferguson, conversation with the author, June 2023.
15. Sabine Junginger, "Towards Policy-Making as Designing: Policy-Making beyond Problem-Solving and Decision-Making," In *Design for Policy*, ed. Christian Bason, 57–69 (New York: Routledge, 2014).
16. *State Plan for the American Rescue Plan Elementary and Secondary School Emergency Relief Fund* (Washington, DC: US Department of Education, 2021).

17. Catherine Durose and Liz Richardson, *Designing Public Policy for Co-Production: Theory, Practice and Change* (Bristol, UK: Policy, 2015), 24.
18. Norman, *The Design of Everyday Things*, 231–32.
19. Cliff Kuang and Robert Fabricant, *User Friendly: How the Hidden Rules of Design Are Changing the Way We Live, Work & Play* (New York: Random House, 2019), 34.
20. Idris Mootee, *Design Thinking for Strategic Innovation: What They Can't Teach You at Business or Design School* (Hoboken, NJ: Wiley, 2013), 150–51.
21. "Don Chadwick, Product Designer," Visionaries on Innovation (Video Oral History Transcript), The Henry Ford, updated August 2, 2009, https://www.thehenryford.org/explore/stories-of-innovation/visionaries/don-chadwick/.
22. Herbert A. Simon, *The Sciences of the Artificial* (Cambridge, MA: MIT Press, 1969).
23. Paul Pierson, "When Effect Becomes Cause: Policy Feedback and Political Change," *World Politics* 45, no. 4 (1993): 622.
24. Norman, *The Design of Everyday Things*, 229–30.
25. Sebastian Sewerin, Daniel Béland, and Benjamin Cashore, "Designing Policy for the Long Term: Agency, Policy Feedback and Policy Change," *Policy Sciences* 53 (2020): 246–47; Benjamin Cashore and Michael Howlett, "Punctuating Which Equilibrium? Understanding Thermostatic Policy Dynamics in Pacific Northwest Forestry," *American Journal of Political Science* 51, no. 3 (2007): 545–46.
26. John M. Bryson, Barbara C. Crosby, and Danbi Seo, "Using a Design Approach to Create Collaborative Governance," *Policy & Politics* 48, no. 1 (2020): 168; Norman, *The Design of Everyday Things*; and "Design Thinking," IDEO, https://designthinking.ideo.com/faq/how-do-people-define-design-thinking.
27. Tyack, *The One Best System: A History of American Urban Education* (Cambridge, MA: Harvard University Press, 1974), 11.
28. Tyack, *The One Best System*, 11.
29. Roger Dean Duncan, "Wouldn't You Like to Solve Just about Anything Fast?," *Forbes Media*, May 1, 2019, https://www.forbes.com/sites/rodgerdeanduncan/2019/05/01/wouldnt-you-like-to-solve-just-about-anything-fast/?sh=3f577d793b07.
30. J. Matthew Bodnar, "Cracking Complexity: This Is How You Solve Your Toughest Problems, with David Komlos & David Benjamin," Science of Success (podcast audio), 2019, https://www.successpodcast.com/show-notes/2019/5/15/cracking-complexity-this-is-how-you-solve-your-toughest-problems-with-david-komlos-amp-david-benjamin.
31. Richard F. Elmore, *Complexity and Control: What Legislators and Administrators Can Do about Implementing Public Policy* (Washington, DC: Office of Education, 1980), 2.
32. Bodnar, "Cracking Complexity."
33. John Naughton, "Ashby's Law of Requisite Variety," Edge, 2017, https://www.edge.org/response-detail/27150.

34. Clarence N. Stone, "Civic Capacity and Urban Education," *Urban Affairs Review* 36, no. 5 (2001): 606.
35. Paul T. Hill, Christine Campbell, and James Harvey, *It Takes a City: Getting Serious about Urban School Reform* (Washington, DC: Brookings Institution Press, 2001), quoted in Clarence N. Stone et al., *Building Civic Capacity: The Politics of Reforming Urban Schools* (University Press of Kansas, 2001), 157.
36. Theo Toonen, "Resilience in Public Administration: The Work of Elinor and Vincent Ostrom from a Public Administration Perspective," *Public Administration Review* 70, no. 2 (2010): 194.
37. Elinor Ostrom, "A Communitarian Approach to Local Governance," *National Civic Review* 82, no. 3 (1993): 232.
38. Ostrom, "A Communitarian Approach to Local Governance."
39. National Center for Education Statistics, *Digest of Education Statistics* (Washington, DC: US Department of Education, Institute of Education Sciences, 2012), https://nces.ed.gov/programs/digest/d12/tables/dt12_098.asp.
40. Martin Gilens and Benjamin I. Page, "Testing Theories of American Politics: Elites, Interest Groups, and Average Citizens," *Perspectives on Politics* 12, no. 3 (2014): 564–81; Emma Vadehra, "We Need to Reimagine the Modern Think Tank," *Stanford Social Innovation Review,* May 27, 2021, https://doi.org/10.48558/2PW0-1548.
41. Elinor Ostrom, "Policy Analysis in the Future of Good Societies," *Good Society* 11, no. 1 (2002): 45.
42. Emma Blomkamp, "The Promise of Co-Design for Public Policy," *Australian Journal of Public Administration* 77, no. 4 (2018): 729–43.
43. Helle Vibeke Carstensen and Christian Bason, "Powering Collaborative Policy Innovation: Can Innovation Labs Help," *Innovation Journal: The Public Sector Innovation Journal* 17, no. 1 (2012): 2–26.
44. Christian Bason, ed., *Design for Policy* (New York: Routledge, 2014), 30–31.
45. Caroline Hill, Michelle Molitor, and Christine Ortiz, *Equityxdesign: A Practice for Transformation* (EquityXDesign Collaborative, 2016), 2.
46. As quoted in John W. Kingdon, *Agendas, Alternatives, and Public Policies*, 2nd ed. (Glenville, IL: Pearson Education, 2010), 2.
47. Amy Gutmann and Dennis Thompson, *Why Deliberative Democracy?* (Princeton, NJ: Princeton University Press, 2004), 9.
48. Gutmann and Thompson, *Why Deliberative Democracy?*; Archon Fung, "Democratizing the Policy Process," in *The Oxford Handbook of Public Policy*, ed. Michael Moran, Martin Rein, and Robert E. Goodin, 669–85 (Oxford: Oxford University Press, 2006); Blomkamp, "The Promise of Co-Design for Public Policy"; and Jenny M. Lewis, Michael McGann, and Emma Blomkamp, "When Design Meets Power: Design Thinking, Public Sector Innovation and the Politics of Policymaking," *Policy & Politics* 48, no. 1 (2020): 111–30.

49. Hill, Molitor, and Ortiz, *Equityxdesign*.
50. Jenny Stewart, *The Dilemmas of Engagement: The Role of Consultation in Governance* (Canberra, Australia: ANU Press, 2009), 4–5.
51. Ibram X. Kendi, *How to Be an Antiracist* (New York: One World, 2019), 18.
52. Kendi, *How to Be an Antiracist*, 18.
53. Hill, Molitor, and Ortiz, *Equityxdesign*, 11.
54. Stephen Page, "A Strategic Framework for Building Civic Capacity," *Urban Affairs Review* 52, no. 4 (2016): 1–32.
55. Blomkamp, "The Promise of Co-Design for Public Policy."
56. Anthony S. Bryk et al., *Learning to Improve: How America's Schools Can Get Better at Getting Better* (Cambrdige, MA: Harvard Education Press, 2015), 3–5.
57. However, later research conducted by MDRC found positive outcomes. See Rebecca Unterman and Zeest Haider, *New York City's Small Schools of Choice: A First Look at Effects on Postsecondary Persistence and Labor Market Outcomes*, MDRC, April 2019, https://www.mdrc.org/sites/default/files/SSC-First_Look%20Brief.pdf.
58. Bryk et al., *Learning to Improve*, 3.
59. Gutmann and Thompson, *Why Deliberative Democracy?*, 12.
60. Robert C. Luskin et al., "Deliberating across Deep Divides," *Political Studies* 62, no. 1 (2014): 116–35.
61. According to Luskin et al., "Deliberating across Deep Divides," 48 percent of schools are state-controlled and represent the Protestant population, and 43 percent of schools are Catholic-maintained.
62. Melissa De Witte, "Could Deliberative Democracy Depolarize America? Stanford Scholars Think So," Stanford News Service, February 4, 2021, https://news.stanford.edu/2021/02/04/deliberative-democracy-depolarize-america/.
63. Anthony S. Bryk et al., *How a City Learned to Improve Its Schools* (Cambridge, MA: Harvard Education Press, 2023), 277–91.
64. Ronald A. Heifetz and Riley M. Sinder, "Political Leadership: Managing the Public's Problem Solving," in *The Power of Public Ideas* (Cambridge, MA: Harvard University Press, 1988), 201.
65. Lucy Kimbell, "Design in the Time of Policy Problems," *Proceedings of DRS2016: Design+ Research+ Society-Future-Focused Thinking* 8 (2016): 2.
66. Jesper Christiansen and Laura Bunt, "Innovating Public Policy: Allowing for Social Complexity and Uncertainty in the Design of Public Outcomes," in *Design for Policy*, ed. Christian Bason (New York: Routledge, 2014), 47.
67. Bason, *Design for Policy*, 163.
68. Lewis, McGann, and Blomkamp, "When Design Meets Power."
69. Simona Maschi and Jennie Winhall, "Tools for Implementation," in *Design for Policy*, ed. Christian Bason, 213–23 (New York: Routledge, 2014).

CHAPTER 4

1. Christopher Ansell, Eva Sørensen, and Jacob Torfing, "Improving Policy Implementation through Collaborative Policymaking," *Policy & Politics* 45, no. 3 (2017): 467–86.
2. Michael Lipsky, *Street-Level Bureaucracy: Dilemmas of the Individual in Public Service* (New York: Russell Sage Foundation, 2010), 13–26.
3. Clarence N. Stone, "Efficiency versus Social Learning: A Reconsideration of the Implementation Process," *Review of Policy Research* 4 (1985): 489.
4. Clarence N. Stone et al., *Building Civic Capacity: The Politics of Reforming Urban Schools* (Lawrence: University Press of Kansas, 2001), 7–8.
5. James P. Spillane, *Standards Deviation: How Schools Misunderstand Education Policy* (Cambridge, MA: Harvard University Press, 2009), 176–78.
6. Richard F. Elmore, *Complexity and Control: What Legislators and Administrators Can Do about Implementing Public Policy* (Washington, DC: Office of Education, 1980); and Richard F. Elmore, "Backward Mapping: Implementation Research and Policy Decisions," *Political Science Quarterly* 94, no. 4 (Winter 1979–1980): 601–16.
7. Elmore, "Backward Mapping," 604.
8. Elmore, *Complexity and Control*, 29–30.
9. Jennie Winhall and Simona Maschi, "Tools for Implementation," in *Design for Policy*, ed. Christian Bason (New York: Routledge, 2014), 213.
10. Ansell, Sørensen, and Torfing, "Improving Policy Implementation through Collaborative Policymaking."
11. Christopher Ansell, Eva Sørensen, and Jacob Torfing, "Improving Policy Implementation Through Collaborative Policymaking," *Policy & Politics Journal* Blog, September 13, 2017, https://policyandpoliticsblog.com/2017/09/13/improving-policy-implementation-through-collaborative-policymaking/.
12. Melissa Roderick, John Q. Easton, and Penny Bender Sebring, *The Consortium on Chicago School Research: A New Model for the Role of Research in Supporting Urban School Reform* (Chicago: Consortium on Chicago School Research at the University of Chicago Urban Education Insitute, February 2009), 25–27.
13. Ansell, Sørensen, and Torfing, "Improving Policy Implementation through Collaborative Policymaking" (journal essay).
14. Maeve P. Carey, *Negotiated Rulemaking: In Brief*, Congressional Research Service, April 12, 2021, https://crsreports.congress.gov. Note: Neg-reg is distinct from the required use of the notice-and-comment process that provides public notice of impending rule changes and allows for public comment before the rule is finalized. The notice-and-comment process would follow after the neg-reg process of creating a consensus proposed rule.

15. Chris Ansell and Alison Gash, "Collaborative Governance in Theory and Practice," *Journal of Public Administration Research and Theory* 18, no. 4 (2008): 553–71.
16. "Issue Paper 3: Gainful Employment Session 1: January 18–21, 2022," Office of Postsecondary Education, U.S. Department of Education, 2022, https://www2.ed.gov/policy/highered/reg/hearulemaking/2021/3gainfulemployment.pdf.
17. John S. Dryzek et al., "The Crisis of Democracy and the Science of Deliberation," *Science* 262, no. 6432 (2019): 1144–46.
18. Elmore, *Complexity and Control*, vi.
19. Elmore, "Backward Mapping," 610.
20. Lawrence Wright's book *The End of October*, published just before the pandemic, and films that took on a similar storyline include *Outbreak* (1995) and *Contagion* (2011). David Quammen, "Why Weren't We Ready for the Coronavirus?," *New Yorker*, May 4, 2020, https://www.newyorker.com/magazine/2020/05/11/why-werent-we-ready-for-the-coronavirus.
21. Lauraine Langreo, "What Educators Think about Using AI in Schools," *Education Week*, April 14, 2023, https://www.edweek.org/technology/what-educators-think-about-using-ai-in-schools/2023/04.
22. Piret Tõnurist and Angela Hanson, "Anticipatory Innovation Governance: Shaping the Future through Proactive Policy Making," *OCED Working Papers on Public Governance*, no. 44 (2020): 34.
23. Azad Singh Bali, Giliberto Capano, and M. Ramesh, "Anticipating and Designing for Policy Effectiveness," *Policy & Society* 38, no. 1 (2019): 1–13; and Milbrey W. McLaughlin, "The Rand Change Agent Study Revisited: Macro Perspectives and Micro Realities," *Educational Researcher* 19, no. 9 (1990): 11–16.
24. Tõnurist and Hanson, "Anticipatory Innovation Governance," 28.
25. Elmore, *Complexity and Control*, 37–39.
26. Meredith I. Honig, "Complexity and Policy Implementation: Challenges and Opportunities for the Field," in *New Directions in Education Policy Implementation*, ed. Meredith I. Honig, 1–23 (New York: SUNY Press, 2006).
27. James P. Spillane, Brian J. Reiser, and Todd Reimer, "Policy Implementation and Cognition: Reframing and Refocusing Implementation Research," *Review of Educational Research* 72, no. 3 (2002): 387–431; Meredith I. Honig, ed., *New Directions in Educational Policy Implementation* (New York: SUNY Press, 2006); and Cynthia E. Coburn, Meredith I. Honig, and Mary Kay Stein, "What's the Evidence on Districts' Use of Evidence," in *The Role of Research in Educational Improvement*, ed. John. D. Bransford et al., 67–87 (Cambridge MA: Harvard Education Press, 2009).
28. Honig, "Complexity and Policy Implementation," 17.
29. Giandomenico Majone, *Evidence, Argument, and Persuasion in the Policy Process* (New Haven, CT: Yale University Press, 1989).

30. Elizabeth Anderson, "The Epistemology of Democracy," *Episteme: A Journal of Social Epistemology* 3, no. 1–2 (2006): 8–22; and Ian Sanderson, "Intelligent Policy Making for a Complex World: Pragmatism, Evidence and Learning," *Political Studies* 57, no. 4 (2009): 699–719.
31. Ansell, Sørensen, and Torfing, "Improving Policy Implementation through Collaborative Policymaking" *Policy & Politics* 45, no. 3 (2017): 467–87 (journal essay).
32. Richard Freeman, "Learning in Public Policy," in *The Oxford Handbook of Public Policy*, ed. Michael Moran, Martin Rein, and Robert E. Goodin, 367–88 (Oxford: Oxford University Press: 2006).
33. Anderson, "The Epistemology of Democracy."
34. Freeman, "Learning in Public Policy."
35. Atul Gawande, "Slow Ideas," *New Yorker*, July 22, 2013, https://www.newyorker.com/magazine/2013/07/29/slow-ideas.
36. Cynthia E. Coburn, Meredith I. Honig, and Mary Kay Stein, "What's the Evidence on Districts' Use of Evidence," in *The Role of Research in Educational Improvement*, ed. John. D. Bransford et al. (Cambridge MA: Harvard Education Press, 2009), 67–87.
37. Spillane, Reiser, and Reimer, "Policy Implementation and Cognition," 387–431.
38. Anderson, "The Epistemology of Democracy," 14.
39. David Cohen and Jal Mehta, "Why Reform Sometimes Succeeds: Understanding the Conditions That Produce Reforms That Last," *American Educational Research Journal* (2017): 644–90.
40. Karl E. Weick, "The Collapse of Sensemaking in Organizations: The Mann Gulch Disaster," *Administrative Science Quarterly* (1993): 628–52.
41. James P. Spillane, *Standards Deviation: How Schools Misunderstand Education Policy* (Cambridge, MA: Harvard University Press, 2006), 93–112.
42. Cliff Kuang and Robert Fabricant, *User Friendly: How the Hidden Rules of Design Are Changing the Way We Live, Work & Play* (New York: MCD, 2019).
43. Majone, *Evidence, Argument, and Persuasion in the Policy Process*, 180–83.
44. Michael Kirst and Richard Jung, "The Utility of a Longitudinal Approach in Assessing Implementation: A Thirteen-Year View of Title I, ESEA," *Educational Evaluation and Policy Analysis* 2, no. 5 (1980): 17.
45. Paul A. Sabatier, "Two Decades of Implementation Research: From Control to Guidance and Learning," *The Public Sector: Challenge for Coordination and Learning* 31 (1991): 257.
46. Donella H. Meadows and Diana Wright, *Thinking in Systems: A Primer* (White River Junction, VT: Chelsea Green, 2008), 23.
47. James J. Heckman et al., *A New Cost-Benefit and Rate of Return Analysis for the Perry Preschool Program: A Summary* (Cambridge, MA: National Bureau of Economic Research, 2010), 1–11.

48. Raj Chetty, Nathaniel Hendren, and Lawrence F. Katz, "The Effects of Exposure to Better Neighborhoods on Children: New Evidence from the Moving to Opportunity Experiment," *American Economic Review* 106, no. 4 (2016): 855–902.
49. The suggestion that it takes time to learn by doing and the example of ESEA evaluation were drawn from Majone, *Evidence, Argument, and Persuasion in the Policy Process*, 180–83.
50. Majone, *Evidence, Argument, and Persuasion in the Policy Process*, 182.
51. Min Sun, Alec I. Kennedy, and Susanna Loeb, "The Longitudinal Effects of School Improvement Grants," *Educational Evaluation and Policy Analysis* 43, no. 4 (2021): 647–67.
52. Ansell, Sørensen, and Torfing, "Improving Policy Implementation through Collaborative Policymaking" (journal essay).
53. Stone et al., *Building Civic Capacity*; Hélène Landemore, *Democratic Reason: Politics, Collective Intelligence, and the Rule of the Many* (Princeton, NJ: Princeton University Press, 2017); Sanderson, "Intelligent Policy Making for a Complex World."
54. Landemore, *Democratic Reason*, 14.
55. James Fishkin et al., "Is Deliberation an Antidote to Extreme Partisan Polarization? Reflections on 'America in One Room,'" *American Political Science Review* 115, no. 4 (2021): 1464–81.
56. Anthony Bryk et al., *Learning to Improve: How America's Schools Can Get Better at Getting Better* (Cambridge, MA: Harvard Education Press, 2015), 1–19.
57. Alain, *Les Propos d'un Normand de 1908* (Klincksieck, 1993), quoted in D. S. Rogers and P. R. Ehrlich, "Natural Selection and Cultural Rates of Change," *Proceedings of the National Academy of Sciences* 105 (2008): 3416–20.
58. Louis Menand, *The Metaphysical Club: A Story of Ideas in America* (New York: Farrar, Straus, and Giroux), 323.
59. Gerry Stoker, "Public Value Management: A New Narrative for Networked Governance?," *American Review of Public Administration* 36, no. 1 (2006): 41–57; and Tõnurist and Hanson, "Anticipatory Innovation Governance."
60. Sanderson, "Intelligent Policy Making for a Complex World."

CHAPTER 5

1. Jessica Paga, "The Agora: Form, Function, and Ideology," in *Building Democracy in Late Archaic Athens*, 77–126 (Oxford: Oxford University Press, 2021).
2. Pedro Henrique H. F. de Cristo, "Digital Agora: A Physical and Digital Space for Participatory Democracy," Paper presented at the Cross-Americas: Probing Disglobal Networks, 2016, https://www.acsa-arch.org/chapter/digital-agora-a-physical-and-digitalspace-for-participatory-democracy/.
3. For a more detailed description of the concrete and symbolic value of buildings for democratic politics described in this section, see Paga, "The Agora."

4. "Health of the U.S. Nonprofit Sector," Independent Sector, October 2020, https://independentsector.org/resource/health-of-the-u-s-nonprofit-sector/.
5. Meredith I. Honig, "The New Middle Management: Intermediary Organizations in Education Policy Implementation," *Educational Evaluation and Policy Analysis* 26, no. 1 (2004): 65–87.
6. Robert B. Reich, ed., *The Power of Public Ideas* (Cambridge, MA: Harvard University Press, 1990), 11.
7. Yannis Papadopoulos, "On the Embeddedness of Deliberative Systems: Why Elitist Innovations Matter More," in *Deliberative Systems: Deliberative Democracy at the Large Scale*, ed. John Parkinson and Jane Mansbridge, 125–50 (Cambridge: Cambridge University Press, 2012).
8. Vivien A. Schmidt, *Democracy in Europe: The EU and National Polities* (Oxford: Oxford University Press, 2006), 28–29.
9. Honig, "The New Middle Management."
10. There are a number of policy-influencing groups that are not included as policy intermediaries in this definition. For example, lobbying organizations and interest groups whose sole purpose is to influence government or social movements, such as Black Lives Matter and the Me Too movement that focus on mobilizing interests and social change campaigns, are not included. These organizations are essential to reform, yet their goal is to activate like-minded people to move on policy rather than to broker policy deliberation. The focus here is on collaborative policy development rather than the powerful and necessary forces of collective action.
11. Honig, "The New Middle Management," 66.
12. Honig, "The New Middle Management"; Jennifer Watling Neal, Zachary P. Neal, and Brian Brutzman, "Defining Brokers, Intermediaries, and Boundary Spanners: A Systematic Review," *Evidence & Policy: A Journal of Research, Debate and Practice* (2021): 7–24.
13. Honig, "The New Middle Management."
14. For additional descriptions of this project, see Joel Knudson et al., "Fostering Innovation: How User-Centered Design Can Help Us Get the Local Control Funding Formula Right," California Collaborative on District Reform, 2017, https://cacollaborative.org/sites/default/files/CA_Collaborative_LCFF_Fostering_Innovation.pdf; Joel Knudson, "User-Centered Design as a Pathway to Effective Policy: Lessons from the LCFF Test Kitchen, California Collaborative on District Reform, February 2019, https://cacollaborative.org/sites/default/files/LCFF_Test_Kitchen_Lessons_Learned.pdf; and Joel Knudson, "Improving LCFF Implementation through User-Centered Design: Year 1 of the LCFF Test Kitchen," California Collaborative on District Reform, February 2019, https://cacollaborative.org/sites/default/files/LCFF_Test_Kitchen_Prototypes.pdf.
15. Julia E. Koppich, Daniel C. Humphrey, and Julie A. Marsh, "Two Years of California's Local Control Funding Formula: Time to Reaffirm the Grand Vision,"

Policy Analysis for California Education, December 2015, https://edpolicyinca.org/sites/default/files/LCFF.pdf.

16. "United We Learn: Hearing Kentucky's Voices on the Future of Education," Kentucky Department of Education, August 30, 2022, https://education.ky.gov/UnitedWeLearn/Pages/default.aspx.
17. "A Citywide Approach to Acceleration: Early Lessons from CityTutor DC, CityTutor DC and CityBridge Education, March 2022, https://issuu.com/citybridgeeducation/docs/ctdc_midyear_report_final_full_with_links_1_?e=45137175/92176131.
18. Rena Johnson in discussion with the author, December 2022.
19. See Justice Louis Brandeis's dissenting opinion in *New State Ice Co. v. Liebmann*, 285 US 262 (1932).
20. Daniel Béland, *How Ideas and Institutions Shape the Politics of Public Policy* (Cambridge: Cambridge University Press, 2019), 15.
21. Charles W. Tyler and Heather K. Gerken, "The Myth of the Laboratories of Democracy," *Columbia Law Review* 122, no. 8 (2022): 2187–240.
22. Tyler and Gerken, "The Myth of the Laboratories of Democracy," 2199.
23. John S. Dryzek, "Democratization as Deliberative Capacity Building," *Comparative Political Studies* 42, no. 11 (2009): 1379–402.
24. Alexander C. Furnas and Timothy M. LaPira, "Congressional Brain Drain: Legislative Capacity in the 21st Century," New America, September 2020), https://www.newamerica.org/political-reform/reports/congressional-brain-drain/congressional-staffers-job-satisfaction-career-trajectories-and-compensation/; Paul Glastris and Haley Sweetland Edwards, "The Big Lobotomy: How Republicans Made Congress Stupid," *Washington Monthly*, June/July/August, 2014, https://washingtonmonthly.com/2014/06/09/the-big-lobotomy/.
25. Furnas and LaPira, "Congressional Brain Drain."
26. Richard F. Elmore, "Backward Mapping: Implementation Research and Policy Decisions," *Political Science Quarterly* 94, no. 4 (Winter 1979–1980): 607.
27. Richard F. Elmore, *Complexity and Control: What Legislators and Administrators Can Do about Implementing Public Policy* (Washington, DC: Office of Education, 1980), 31.
28. David Tyack and William Tobin, "The 'Grammar' of Schooling: Why Has It Been So Hard to Change?," *American Educational Research Journal* 31, no. 3 (1994): 479.
29. Martin Jones and Joyce Liddle, "Implementing the UK Central Government's Policy Agenda for Improved Third Sector Engagement: Reflecting on Issues Arising from Third Sector Commissioning Workshops," *International Journal of Public Sector Management* (2011): 160.
30. Lu Hong and Scott E. Page, "Groups of Diverse Problem Solvers Can Outperform Groups of High-Ability Problem Solvers," *Proceedings of the National Academy of Sciences* 101, no. 46 (2004): 16385–89.

31. David Estlund and Hélène Landemore, "The Epistemic Value of Democratic Deliberation," in *The Oxford Handbook of Deliberative Democracy*, ed. Andre Bächtiger et al., 113–31 (Oxford: Oxford Academic, 2018).
32. Clarence N. Stone et al., *Building Civic Capacity: The Politics of Reforming Urban Schools*, (Lawrence: University Press of Kansas, 2001).
33. Reich, *The Power of Public Ideas*, 3–7.
34. Frances Fox Piven and Richard Cloward, *Poor People's Movements: Why They Succeed, How They Fail* (New York: Vintage Books, 2012); and Mary Kaldor, "Civil Society and Accountability," *Journal of Human Development* 4, no. 1 (2003): 5–27.
35. Olaf Corry, "Defining and Theorizing the Third Sector," in *Third Sector Research*, ed. Rupert Taylor, 11–20 (New York: Springer 2010).
36. Sarah Reckhow, Davia Downey, and Joshua Sapotichne, "Governing without Government: Nonprofit Governance in Detroit and Flint," *Urban Affairs Review* 56, no. 5 (2020): 1472–502; and Douglas N. Harris, *Charter School City: What the End of Traditional Public Schools in New Orleans Means for American Education* (Chicago: University of Chicago Press, 2020).
37. Reckhow et al., "Governing without Government."
38. Robert E. Goodin, "Democratic Accountability: The Distinctiveness of the Third Sector," *European Journal of Sociology/Archives Européennes de Sociologie* 44, no. 3 (2003): 359–96; and Yannis Papadopoulos, "Problems of Democratic Accountability in Network and Multilevel Governance," *European Law Journal* 13, no. 4 (2007): 469–86.
39. Goodin, "Democratic Accountability."
40. Margaret Talbot, "The Increasingly Wild World of School-Board Meetings," *New Yorker*, October 8, 2021, https://www.newyorker.com/news/daily-comment/the-increasingly-wild-world-of-school-board-meetings.
41. Adam Laats, "School Board Meetings Used to Be Boring. Why Have They Become War Zones?," *Washington Post*, September 29, 2021, https://www.washingtonpost.com/outlook/2021/09/29/school-board-meetings-used-be-boring-why-have-they-become-war-zones/; and Brian W. Jones, "Furious Parents at School Board Meetings Have a Right to Speak. We Should Listen to Them," *Washington Post*, October 13 2021, https://www.washingtonpost.com/opinions/2021/10/13/angry-parents-school-board-meetings-dissent-free-speech/.
42. John S. Dryzek et al., "The Crisis of Democracy and the Science of Deliberation," *Science* 363, no. 6432 (2019): 1144–46.

CHAPTER 6

1. William G. Howell, "Results of President Obama's Race to the Top," *Education Next* 15, no. 4 (2015): 58–67.

2. Race to the Top used a similar style of back-and-forth interaction in working with states to implement the policy's expectations but was originally a competition with winners and losers, whereas the NCLB waivers program expected to grant flexibility to all states. Still, Race to the Top holds lessons for a reconsiderd federalism, particularly in the creation of individual state implementation support.
3. David J. Barron and Todd D. Rakoff, "In Defense of Big Waiver," *Columbia Law Review* (2013): 265–345; Samuel R. Bagenstos, "Federalism by Waiver after the *Health Care Case*," in *The Health Care Case: The Supreme Court's Decision and Its Implications*, ed. Gillian Metzger, Trevor Morrison, and Nathaniel Persily, 227–44 (Oxford: Oxford Academic, 2013).
4. Barron and Rakoff, "In Defense of Big Waiver."
5. *Every Student Succeeds Act*, 20 USC. § 6301 (2015), Part A, subpart 1, section 1111(b)(G)(ii).
6. Heather K. Gerken, "Federalism and Nationalism: Time for a Détente," *St. Louis University Law Journal* 59 (2015): 997–1044.
7. Kimberly Jenkins Robinson, "Disrupting Education Federalism," *Washington University Law Review* 92 (2014): 959.
8. In 2017–2018, federal support for public elementary and secondary schools as a percent of total school funding ranged from a low of 4.1 percent in New Jersey to a high of 15.9 percent in Alaska. The average federal portion of total school funding was 7.8 percent across fifty states and the District of Columbia. Data are available at National Center for Education Statistics, "Public School Revenue Sources," 2022, https://nces.ed.gov/programs/coe/indicator/cma.
9. Susan H. Fuhrman, Margaret E. Goertz, and Elliot H. Weinbaum, "Educational Governance in the United States: Where Are We? How Did We Get Here? Why Should We Care?," in *The State of Education Policy Research*, ed. David K. Cohen, Susan H. Fuhrman, and Fritz Mosher, 41–61 (Mahwah, NJ: Lawrence Erlbaum Associates, 2007).
10. Frederick M. Hess and Andrew P. Kelly, eds., *Carrots, Sticks, and the Bully Pulpit: Lessons from a Half-Century of Federal Efforts to Improve America's Schools* (Cambridge, MA: Harvard Education Press, 2012), 1.
11. "White House Report: The Every Student Succeeds Act," White House Office of the Press Secretary, December 10, 2015, https://obamawhitehouse.archives.gov/the-press-office/2015/12/10/white-house-report-every-student-succeeds-act.
12. Jessica Bulman-Pozen and Heather K. Gerken, "Uncooperative Federalism," *Yale Law Journal* 118 (2008): 1256–310; and Gerken, "Federalism and Nationalism."
13. Many terms are used to describe similar approaches: polyphonic federalism, cooperative federalism, negotiated federalism, relational federalism, and new federalism. For further information, see Heather K. Gerken, "Federalism 3.0,"

California Law Review 105 (2017): 1695–723. I have chosen the term "relational federalism" to emphasize the human connections rather than just institutional interactions as well as to avoid the suggestion within the term "cooperative federalism" that it is cooperation rather than contention that improves policies. On the contrary, disputes are often critical.

14. Robert A. Schapiro, "Toward a Theory of Interactive Federalism," *Iowa Law Review* 91 (2005): 243–49.
15. Heather K. Gerken, "Foreword: Federalism All the Way Down," *Harvard Law Review* 124, no. 1 (2010): 4–74; Gerken, "Federalism and Nationalism"; and Abbe R. Gluck, "Federalism from Federal Statutes: Health Reform, Medicaid, and the Old-Fashioned Federalists' Gamble," *Fordham Law Review* 81 (2012): 1749–75.
16. Gerken, "Federalism 3.0," 1703.
17. Archon Fung, "Four Levels of Power: A Conception to Enable Liberation," *Journal of Political Philosophy* 28, no. 2 (2020): 131–57.
18. Gerken, "Federalism and Nationalism." The description of cooperative, relational federalism has largely been developed by legal scholars. Scholars in this tradition argue that US courts ought to consider the reality of federal-state integration and interplay when deciding court cases over rights and authority. See Gerken, "Foreword"; Gerken, "Federalism and Nationalism"; Bulman-Pozen and Gerken, "Uncooperative Federalism"; Gluck, "Federalism from Federal Statutes"; Gillian E. Metzger, "Federalism under Obama," *William & Mary Law Review* 53 (2011): 567–619; Schapiro, "Toward a Theory of Interactive Federalism."
19. Schapiro, "Toward a Theory of Interactive Federalism."
20. Gerken, "Federalism 3.0."
21. Michael Lipsky, *Street-Level Bureaucracy: Dilemmas of the Individual in Public Service* (New York: Russell Sage Foundation, 2010).
22. Schapiro, "Toward a Theory of Interactive Federalism," 249.
23. Gerken, "Foreword."
24. The data in this paragraph is from Condition of Education reports prepared by the National Center for Education Statistics, including the following: "Public Charter School Enrollment," National Center for Education Statistics, 2022, https://nces.ed.gov/programs/coe/indicator/cgb/public-charter-enrollment; "Homeschooled Children and Reasons for Homeschooling," National Center for Education Statistics, 2022, https://nces.ed.gov/programs/coe/indicator/tgk/homeschooled-children; and "Private School Enrollment," National Center for Education Statistics, 2022, https://nces.ed.gov/programs/coe/indicator/cgc/private-school-enrollment.
25. Gerken, "Foreword."
26. Richard F. Elmore, "Complexity and Control: What Legislators and Administrators Can Do about Implementing Public Policy," Office of Education, 1980, https://files.eric.ed.gov/fulltext/ED199906.pdf.

27. Chad Aldeman, Kelly Robson, and Andy Smarick, *Pacts Americana: Balancing National Interests, State Autonomy, and Education Accountability* (Sudbury, MA: Bellwether Education Partners, June 2015), 24.
28. Schapiro, "Toward a Theory of Interactive Federalism."
29. Gerken, "Federalism and Nationalism."
30. Daniel Béland and Valéry Ridde, "Ideas and Policy Implementation: Understanding the Resistance against Free Health Care in Africa," *Global Health Governance* 10, no. 3 (2016): 9–23.
31. Lipsky, *Street-Level Bureaucracy*.
32. Lucy Gilson, "Michael Lipsky, Street-Level Bureaucracy: Dilemmas of the Individual in Public Service," in *The Oxford Handbook of Classics in Public Policy and Administration*, ed. Steven J. Balla, Martin Lodge, and Edward C. Page, 383–404 (Oxford: Oxford University Press, 2015).
33. Gilson, "Michael Lipsky, Street-Level Bureaucracy."
34. Gerken, "Federalism 3.0," 1706.
35. Gerken, "Federalism 3.0."
36. Schapiro, "Toward a Theory of Interactive Federalism."
37. Metzger, "Federalism under Obama."
38. Aldeman, Robson, and Smarick, *Pacts Americana*, 19.

CHAPTER 7

1. *United We Learn: Transforming Educational Opportunity for Kentucky's Youth through the Creation and Scaling of Competency-based Assessment and Accountability* (Frankfort: Kentucky Department of Education, April 30, 2022), https://oese.ed.gov/files/2022/08/KentuckyCGSA2022application_Redacted.pdf.
2. Eliot A. Cohen, "The Return of Statecraft: Back to Basics in the Post-American World," *Foreign Affairs* 101, no. 3 (May/June 2022): 117–29; Dennis Ross, "Remember Statecraft? What Diplomacy Can Do, and Why We Need it More Than Ever," *American Scholar* 76, no. 3 (2007): 47–57.
3. Robert B. Reich, "Policy Making in a Democracy," in *The Power of Public Ideas*, ed. Robert B. Reich, 123–56 (Cambridge, MA: Harvard University Press, 1990).
4. John Dewey, *The Public and Its Problems: An Essay in Political Inquiry* (Athens: Ohio University Press, 2016), 225.
5. Alice M. Rivlin, *Systematic Thinking for Social Action* (Washington, DC: Brookings Institution Press, 2015).
6. Rivlin, *Systematic Thinking for Social Action*, 67.
7. Robert B. Reich, ed., *The Power of Public Ideas* (Cambridge, MA: Harvard University Press, 1990), 6.
8. Cohen, "The Return of Statecraft."
9. Rivlin, *Systematic Thinking for Social Action*, xiii.
10. Rivlin, *Systematic Thinking for Social Action*, 101.

11. "Reinventing the Policy Ph.D.: The Pardee RAND Redesign," Pardee RAND Graduate School, https://www.pardeerand.edu/degree-program/redesign.html.
12. "Statement on Education for Public Problem Solving," Freeman Spogli Institute for International Studies, Stanford University, 2020, https://fsi.stanford.edu/publicproblemsolving/docs/statement-education-public-problem-solving.
13. "Statement on Education for Public Problem Solving."
14. "Reinventing the Policy Ph.D."
15. Francis Fukuyama, "What's Wrong with Public Policy Education," The American Interest, August 1, 2018, https://www.the-american-interest.com/2018/08/01/whats-wrong-with-public-policy-education/.
16. Anne L. Schneider and Helen M. Ingram, *Policy Design for Democracy* (Lawrence: University Press of Kansas, 1997), 67.
17. Reich, "Policy Making in a Democracy."
18. Schneider and Ingram, *Policy Design for Democracy*, 7.
19. Lester M. Salamon, "The New Governance and the Tools of Public Action: An Introduction," *Fordham Urban Law Journal* 28 (2000): 1611–74.
20. Jenny M. Lewis, Michael McGann, and Emma Blomkamp, "When Design Meets Power: Design Thinking, Public Sector Innovation and the Politics of Policymaking," *Policy & Politics* 48, no. 1 (2020): 11–130.
21. Lee S. Shulman, "Signature Pedagogies in the Professions," *Daedalus* 134, no. 3 (2005): 52–59.
22. Jesper Christiansen and Laura Bunt, "Innovating Public Policy: Allowing for Social Complexity and Uncertainty in the Design of Public Outcomes," in *Design for Policy*, ed. Christian Bason, 41–56 (London: Routledge, 2014).
23. Doannie Tran and Paul Leather in conversation with the author, November 2022.
24. Lisa Blomgren Bingham, Tina Nabatchi, and Rosemary O'Leary, "The New Governance: Practices and Processes for Stakeholder and Citizen Participation in the Work of Government," *Public Administration Review* 65, no. 5 (2005): 547–58; Ronald A. Heifetz and Riley M. Sinder, "Political Leadership: Managing the Public's Problem Solving," in *The Power of Public Ideas*, ed. Robert B. Reich, 179–203 (Cambridge, MA: Harvard University Press, 1988); Salamon, "The New Governance and the Tools of Public Action."
25. Elinor Ostrom, "Policy Analysis in the Future of Good Societies," *Good Society* 11, no. 1 (2002): 45.
26. Reich, *The Power of Public Ideas*, 3–7.
27. Lewis, McGann, and Blomkamp, "When Design Meets Power."
28. Giandomenico Majone, *Evidence, Argument, and Persuasion in the Policy Process* (New Haven, CT: Yale University Press, 1989), 184.
29. Majone, *Evidence, Argument, and Persuasion in the Policy Process*, 183.

CHAPTER 8

1. Clarence N. Stone et al., *Building Civic Capacity: The Politics of Reforming Urban Schools* (Lawrence: University Press of Kansas, 2001), 1–9.
2. Idris Mootee, *Design Thinking for Strategic Innovation: What They Can't Teach You at Business or Design School* (Hoboken, NJ: Wiley, 2013), 150–51.
3. Meredith I. Honig, "Building Policy from Practice: District Central Office Administrators' Roles and Capacity for Implementing Collaborative Education Policy," *Educational Administration Quarterly* 39, no. 3 (2003): 292–338.
4. James P. Spillane, Brian J. Reiser, and Louis M. Gomez, "Policy Implementation and Cognition," in *New Directions in Educational Policy Implementation*, ed. Meredith I. Honig, 47–64 (New York: SUNY Press, 2006).
5. Jeffrey R. Henig, *The End of Exceptionalism in American Education: The Changing Politics of School Reform* (Cambridge, MA: Harvard Education Press, 2013), 164.
6. Heather K. Gerken, "Federalism and Nationalism: Time for a Détente," *St. Louis University Law Journal* 59 (2015): 997–1044.

Acknowledgments

IN CRITIQUING EDUCATION POLICYMAKING, I purposely avoid critiquing the people involved. I have tremendous respect for the policymakers I had the opportunity to work beside. They are smart, passionate, hardworking colleagues with whom I learned the ins and outs of policymaking as we sought to improve education for students across the nation. I honor their work even as I question how we all might have done it differently.

A handful of people in particular have helped me think through important questions and offered insightful and helpful comments in their reading of sections of the book. My appreciation to George Washington University colleagues Jennifer Clayton, Josh Glazer, and Matt Shirrell. Laura Groth buoyed me up with regular walks, thoughtful questions, and great edits. Maria Ferguson helped me pull it all together with her wonderful ability to see the big picture and suggest the right phrase to make meaning of a mess of details.

I thank the people who contributed stories and experiences. My conversations with these colleagues were filled with the ideas and good energy that come with knowing that we are all working it out together. My thanks to Chad Aldeman, Ilene Berman, Syd Dickson, Khalilah Harris, Rena Johnson, Janalee Jordan-Meldrum, Jim Kohlmoos, Joel Knudson, Paul Leather, Landon Mascareñez, Vince Meldrum, Carol McElvain, Arthur McKee, Lillian Pace, Alexandra Pardo, Danica Petroshius, Arun Ramanathan, Patrick Riccards, Elizabeth Ross, Erin Roth, Scott Sargrad, Clarence Stone, Doannie Tran, and Joanne Weiss.

I am grateful to friends and educators who shaped my thinking with their contributions to students and to education, including Mary Blatch, Noel Bravo, Robin Cleveland, Sharon Dannels, Michael Feuer, Meg Holland,

Laura Jimenez, Mark Jordan, Amira Kamara, Claire Libert, Sevinj Mammadova, Rashmi Narsana, Suraj Patel, Andrew Patricio, Mark Schneider, Kelly Stuart, Rebecca Thessin, and Rebecca Wolfe.

And I am grateful to my students at George Washington University, particularly those I had the privilege to teach in Azerbaijan, who are exceptionally able and earnest in their efforts to learn and to make a difference; they will certainly do so.

My admiration and appreciation to the team at the Harvard Education Press. Editor-in-chief Jayne Fargnoli provided heartening support and perceptive edits, along with firm encouragement to include fewer policy abstractions and more policy practicality. Caroline Chauncey gave me an early nudge, thankfully. My thanks to the proposal reviewers who provided generous and generative feedback that greatly improved my early ideas. Thank you also to the production team.

Every aspiring writer needs a friend like Erica Brown. She got me started by declaring that writing a book is possible and kept me going by demanding pages and updates. I wouldn't have gotten far without her relentless good humor, easy wisdom, and most importantly, her friendship. Thank you, Erica.

And finally, to friends and family who enrich life by adding joy and love and laughter, my grateful thanks.

About the Author

ELIZABETH GRANT is superintendent of schools for the Salt Lake City School District. She is a former associate professor of education at George Washington University's Graduate School of Education and Human Development. Grant's formative policy experiences centered in Washington, D.C., where she served at the US Department of Education as a senior policy adviser and chief of staff to the assistant secretary in the Office of Elementary and Secondary Education. The experience was a hands-on lesson in the complexities of making policy. Grant later worked as vice president of education at the American Institutes for Research and as senior vice president at Jobs for the Future. Earlier, she was an education fellow in the office of US senator Patty Murray. Grant worked in schools for more than a dozen years serving as an elementary school principal and a junior high and high school teacher. She is a graduate of the University of Utah and received her MEd from Harvard University and her MA in sociology and PhD in education policy from Stanford University.

Index